From the Garden of Eden to the Manger in Bethlehem

Discovering the Heart of Christmas—A Guided Christian Meditation on Jesus, God's Plan of Redemption, and the True Meaning of the Season

Only One Life

Copyright Page

Dedication

*F*or every heart longing to see Jesus more clearly. May
these meditations draw you closer to the Promise who
became flesh.

Epigraph

"The people that walked in darkness have seen a great light: they that dwell in the land of the shadow of death, upon them hath the light shined." — Isaiah 9:2

Contents

Introduction: The Journey of the Promise

T ake a slow breath in... and gently let it out. Let your heart grow still.

The story of Christmas does not begin in Bethlehem. It begins with a promise.

That promise was God's promise to send His Son—Jesus—the One who would become flesh and live among us.

A promise spoken long ago, when the world first felt the weight of sorrow and fear. In that moment, God whispered hope — a Savior would come.

That promise glowed like a tiny flame in the dark. It passed from generation to generation, flickering, blazing, but never dying. Always moving forward... until it found its home in a manger.

For the next twenty-five days, we will walk with that promise. Each step will bring us closer to Bethlehem, closer to Jesus, closer to the heart of Christmas.

This is your journey too. So breathe deeply. Let go of hurry. Open your heart. The story begins now.

How to Use This Meditation

This book is different from a devotional. There are no activities to complete, no maps to print, no markers to move. Instead, you are invited to pause, imagine, and enter the story of God's promise with your heart and mind.

When you read phrases such as *"close your eyes"* or *"take a breath,"* know that these are gentle cues — not strict instructions. They are simple invitations to slow down, relax, and picture the scene more vividly. Feel free to adapt them in whatever way works best for you.

Each day includes:

- **Meditation Reading** – a guided reflection using Scripture and imagination to draw you into the story.

- **Breath or Visualization Cue** – short prompts to help you settle your heart and picture the scene.

- **Prayer or Praise** – a closing response that always begins and ends with thanks, worship, or adoration.

- **Declaration** – a bold two-sentence truth to carry with you into your day.

Think of this as a journey on the inside. In the devotional, children move a marker closer to the manger. Here, your steps are traced within your heart. With each reading, with each breath, you are walking nearer to Bethlehem — nearer to the manger — nearer to Jesus Himself.

A Word to Parents

If you are reading this with children, do not worry about how perfectly they follow along. Some may close their eyes, others may peek or giggle. That is okay. The goal is not silence or stillness but **God's presence**—letting His promise touch their hearts in a way they can understand.

Encourage them to imagine freely. Let them picture the garden, the manger, the light of the promise in their own way. Trust that the Holy Spirit is planting seeds of wonder and faith through these quiet moments.

Above all, remember: every word of this story points to Jesus. He is the Promise who became flesh—the light shining in the dark, the heart of Christmas.

Day 1: The First Promise

"And I will put enmity between thee and the woman, and between thy seed and her seed; it shall bruise thy head, and thou shalt bruise his heel." — Genesis 3:15

T ake a deep breath in... and slowly let it out. Feel your shoulders relax. Let your hands rest quietly in your lap. Picture yourself stepping into a story that began long ago.

Imagine a garden — the very first garden, Eden itself. The grass is cool beneath your feet, thick and soft like a green carpet. The air smells fresh, like flowers just opening after rain. Birds sing high and clear from the branches above. A gentle breeze touches your face, warm and safe. In this garden, everything is perfect. There is no sadness. No fear. No hiding. Adam and Eve walk with God like a friend, talking with Him in the light of day.

But then... a shadow slips in. It doesn't shout. It whispers. *"Maybe God doesn't really love you. Maybe His way isn't the best."* Adam and Eve listen to the whisper. They take the fruit. They disobey. And in that moment, everything changes.

Now picture a line of tall dominoes, standing in the sunlight — bright and straight. One tips over. Slowly at first... then faster, faster, until they all tumble down in a crashing wave. That's what happened when Adam and Eve sinned.

The world itself feels broken. The garden that once sang with life grows heavy and still. The birds fall silent. The air feels cold. The trees seem to bow in sorrow. Adam and Eve run to hide, their hearts pounding with fear and shame. *Stop and feel that for a moment. The world is no longer* whole. Darkness is spreading like a storm. Everything good feels like it might be lost. What will happen now?

Listen... do you hear it? In the stillness, God is speaking. Not in anger, not in thunder, but with a strong and steady voice, full of love. And you are close enough to hear every word:

"And I will put enmity between thee and the woman, and between thy seed and her seed; it shall bruise thy head, and thou shalt bruise his heel."

These words are not just for Adam and Eve. They are for the whole world. They are for you. Right there in the darkness, God makes a promise. One day, someone will come — a Savior — to crush the serpent's head, to break the power of sin, to bring light back into the world. This was the very first promise of Christmas. That promise was God's promise to send His Son—Jesus—the One who would become flesh and live among us.

That promise never went away. It moved through history like a golden thread, shining in the darkest nights. Sometimes it flickered like a lantern far away. Sometimes it blazed like a fire that could not be put out. But it always pointed forward... forward to a manger in Bethlehem.

This book is the journey of that promise. From the Garden to the Manger, we will follow it step by step, watching the light grow brighter each day. Tonight, you take your very first step. Imagine that promise glowing before you, like a star that never fades. *Breathe it in slowly — hope, love, joy. Breathe out gently — fear, worry, doubt.* With every breath, you are walking closer to the manger, where God's promise will be fulfilled in Jesus.

Tonight, you take your very first step. The story of God's promise begins here — in the garden, where light first broke through the darkness. Today, you see hope shining for the very first time, a promise that will carry us forward toward Bethlehem, toward the manger, and toward Jesus.

Father, thank You for Your first promise—a light shining in the darkness, a hope that never fades. I praise You because even when the world was broken, You gave us a Savior. Help me to trust Your love, even when I feel afraid or unsure. Thank You that Your promise is alive in me, filling me with peace and joy. In Jesus' name. Amen.

I am part of God's promise. Jesus is the light that shines forever. I walk toward the manger with hope, love, and peace in my heart.

Day 2: The Blessing Passed On

"Now the LORD had said unto Abram, Get thee out of thy country, and from thy kindred, and from thy father's house, unto a land that I will shew thee: And I will make of thee a great nation, and I will bless thee, and make thy name great; and thou shalt be a blessing: And I will bless them that bless thee, and curse him that curseth thee: and in thee shall all families of the earth be blessed." — Genesis 12:1–3

*T*ake a deep breath in... hold it... now let it out slowly. Feel your heart grow quiet, your mind becoming still.

Now imagine the early morning desert. The air is cool. The ground beneath your feet is soft with sand. The world is silent except for a faint wind that brushes across your face.

Abram stands beside you, looking out across the empty land. Behind him is everything familiar — his home, his friends, his family. Ahead of him is a road with no clear ending, only a promise.

Listen carefully. God's voice speaks clear and strong: "*Leave your country. Leave your family. I will show you a new land. I will make you a great nation. I will bless you, and you will be a blessing. Through you, all families of the earth will be blessed.*"

Abram swallows hard. His heart beats fast. It is not easy to leave everything behind. But he lifts his foot and takes a step into the unknown, trusting the One who called him.

Look down at your own feet. Slowly imagine lifting one foot... then stepping forward beside Abram. You are walking with him. You are stepping into the promise too.

Abram's yes to God was the start of a blessing that would grow far beyond him. Picture him holding a tiny seed in his hand. Watch as it falls into the earth. From that seed comes a green shoot... then a tree... then a mighty tree with wide branches, leaves shimmering in the light.

This tree is God's blessing. At its heart is Jesus — the greatest blessing of all. His arms are like branches stretching wide, reaching every nation, every family, every child. Reaching out to you.

Stand beneath this tree. Feel the cool shade covering you like a safe shelter. Hear the rustle of the leaves — they whisper hope, peace, joy, love.

Breathe in deeply — God's blessing is for you. Breathe out slowly — let go of your fear.

Just as Abram said yes to God's call, you too can say yes — yes to Jesus, God's greatest promise.

The Bible says: "*That if thou shalt confess with thy mouth the Lord Jesus, and shalt believe in thine heart that God hath raised him from the dead, thou shalt be saved. For with the heart man believeth unto righteousness; and with the mouth confession is made unto salvation.*" — Romans 10:9–10

Place your hand gently on your chest. Feel your heartbeat. Whisper softly: "*I believe in my heart that Jesus is Lord. I believe He died and rose again. I confess with my mouth that He is my Savior. I say yes to Jesus.*"

This first yes is the most important one of all—it's the moment you are saved. When you said yes to Jesus, He forgave your sins and came to live in your heart. You belong to Him now. You are His child forever.

But the journey does not stop here. Just as Abram kept walking day by day, we keep saying yes—not to be saved again, but to follow in trust and obedience. Each step becomes a yes: yes to God's Word, yes to His ways, yes to living in His love.

Now picture yourself back on the desert road. Abram walks ahead, and you walk beside him. Above, the branches of the great tree stretch wide across the sky, its leaves glowing softly with God's promise. The night air is cool, and the path beneath your feet feels steady, even though you cannot yet see the end.

Take a slow breath. With every breath you are walking closer to Bethlehem, closer to the manger where God's greatest promise will be fulfilled.

Yesterday, you stood in the garden and heard God's very first promise — a light shining in the darkness.

Today, you walk beside Abram on a desert road, watching God's blessing stretch wide like a tree whose branches reach every nation. With each step, the promise grows clearer: all of it is leading toward Bethlehem, toward the manger, toward Jesus.

My Father, thank You for the promise You gave to Abram. I praise You for sending Jesus—the greatest blessing to all families of the earth. Thank You for the gift of salvation and for making me part of that promise. Help me to keep saying yes to Your Word, yes to Your ways, and yes to following You every day. I thank You because Your blessing is with me always. In Jesus' name. Amen.

I have said yes to Jesus—He is my Savior and my Lord. Each day I will say yes to His Word and walk in His blessing. I am part of God's promise, moving forward with hope and joy. I am blessed to be a blessing. God's love in me reaches others with His light.

Day 3 — God With Us

"And the Word was made flesh, and dwelt among us, (and we beheld his glory, the glory as of the only begotten of the Father,) full of grace and truth." — John 1:14

C lose *your eyes gently. Let your hands rest loosely in your lap. Take a slow, deep breath, as though you're pulling fresh air into every corner of your lungs. Hold it for a heartbeat... and now let it out slowly, soft and steady, like a breeze sighing through tall grass.*

Breathe again, slower this time. With each exhale, let your shoulders sink. Let the noise within you quiet. Let your heart settle like water after a storm.

Now imagine the night sky over Bethlehem. Darkness stretches like a velvet blanket, pierced by diamonds of starlight scattered in every direction. The air is cool, crisp, carrying the faint smell of smoke from nearby fires. The village lies still, asleep.

And then—within a simple stable, heavy with the smell of hay and the gentle rustling of animals—silence is broken. A cry pierces the night. A baby's cry.

This is no ordinary baby. This is Jesus. The Word made flesh. God wrapped in the soft folds of cloth, His tiny chest rising and falling, His hands curling into fists of newborn strength. The Infinite, lying in a manger. The Creator, breathing among His creation.

Pause here. Whisper softly in your heart: Emmanuel. God with us.

See Him now as a little boy. His laughter rings out as He runs through the dusty streets, sandals slipping against stone. He plays, He learns, He listens. Joseph's strong hands guide His smaller ones over wood and tools, teaching Him to shape and to build.

Picture Him as a man, His feet carrying Him across the Galilean hills. The roads are dusty, but His steps are steady. Watch Him touch a blind man's eyes and see sight return like dawn breaking. Watch Him gather children in His arms, their giggles filling the air as His embrace whispers, *You are safe, you are loved.* Listen as He tells stories—parables that open windows in people's hearts, helping them glimpse what God is really like. Everywhere He goes, heaven touches earth.

But then the air grows heavy. The road shifts. A wooden cross is placed upon His back, and He begins the slow climb up a hill. The wood bites into His skin. His shoulders strain. Each step is agony, yet each step is love. Nails pierce His hands and feet. The sky darkens, heavy clouds rolling in as if creation itself cannot bear the sight. The world feels broken again, like a clay jar smashed upon the ground. His friends weep bitterly, convinced that God with us has slipped away.

Hold this silence for a moment. Let yourself feel the weight of it.

But three days later, everything changes. Light bursts into the darkness. The stone is rolled away. Life surges back into a world that thought it had been abandoned. Jesus steps out of the tomb, radiant, alive, unshakable. Death cannot hold Him. Sin bows before Him. God with us—forever.

Now open your eyes in your imagination and see yourself standing with the disciples on a hillside just outside Jerusalem. The sun is warm against your face. Dust clings to your sandals. The air hums with expectancy—you can almost feel hearts beating faster around you.

Jesus turns toward His friends. His gaze sweeps over them, and His eyes—yes, His eyes—find you too. They are eyes full of steady love, the same love that has followed you from Bethlehem to this very moment. His voice is soft, but it carries weight:

"I will not leave you alone. I will ask the Father, and He will send you the Helper—the Holy Spirit—to be with you forever."

You lean in close, afraid to miss even a syllable. His promise feels like treasure being placed in your open hands. You whisper under your breath: *God with us... still with us.*

Then He lifts His hands, blessing pours from His lips, and joy lights His face. Slowly His feet rise from the earth. Higher, higher, until the sky swallows Him like a brilliant star ascending. Your eyes strain, refusing to blink. You do not want to lose sight of Him.

Suddenly, two figures in shining white are standing right beside you. Their voices are both kind and strong:'*Why are you looking up into the sky? This same Jesus, who has been taken from you, will come back again.*'

Days later, you gather with the disciples in an upper room in Jerusalem. The door is closed, bolted shut. The room is thick with prayers, whispers, and the sound of waiting hearts. You are waiting too—for the promise Jesus gave.

Then—without warning—it happens.

A sound like rushing wind bursts through the house. It is fierce, yet not destructive. It rattles the door, shakes the shutters, swirls around the room until it feels as though the house itself is breathing. Your clothes are tugged, your hair is lifted. You gasp for air, but the very breath around you feels alive—as if God Himself has wrapped you in His presence.

Then your eyes widen. A dove, white as snow, glides through the swirling wind. Its wings beat steady, scattering feathers that fall like gentle snowflakes, brushing your cheeks, resting light as a whisper on your shoulders. It hovers, then dissolves into the wind, leaving the room trembling with holy stillness.

And then—fire.

Flames appear, gentle yet fierce, flickering above each person's head. You see Peter frozen in wonder, his eyes wide beneath the hovering flame. John laughs, a sound of awe caught in his throat. You turn in circles—yes, above every head, the fire dances.

Then you notice it—above you too. A flame glowing, steady, golden. It does not burn. It warms. It fills. It seeps deep into your chest like sunlight, chasing shadows you didn't know were there.

Your lips begin to tremble. Sounds you've never learned press at the edge of your tongue. Around you, voices rise—languages never studied, flowing in worship. The air is filled with praise, each word lifted like a banner of heaven.

Take a deep breath. And now, let your imagination flow into faith and reality. Whisper with me:

Holy Spirit, what I am imagining now—let it come alive in me.Come, Holy Spirit, live inside me.Be my Helper, my Friend, my Teacher.Fill me with fire that burns bright,with wind that makes me strong,with Your gentle voice that guides me every day.Wrap me in Your love like a warm blanket.I open my heart to You.I receive You now. In Jesus' name, Amen.

When you prayed those words, you opened the door wide for **the Holy Spirit** to come and live inside you. That very moment, **He stepped into your heart to stay—God's Spirit Himself, your forever Helper and Friend.**

Don't be afraid of the sound that rises. It may feel new or surprising, but it is from God. It is His Spirit praying through you. You are not making it up—it is a gift, a song of heaven inside you. Breathe in, breathe out, and let Him flow. He is here. He is with you. He is in you.

Take a slow breath now, right where you are. Imagine that same Spirit filling your heart even today. He is not far away. He is close—closer than your own breath.

That is what Christmas means. When Jesus was born, God came to live with us. And even now, through the Holy Spirit, God still lives with us. Emmanuel. God with us—forever.

Yesterday, you walked with Abram beneath the wide branches of God's blessing, watching His promise stretch across the nations.

Today, you stand in Bethlehem and beyond, seeing the promise fulfilled — Jesus born among us, living, dying, rising, and sending His Spirit to dwell within us. The promise has a name: Emmanuel. God with us, forever.

Heavenly Father, thank You for sending Jesus to be with us. Thank You also for giving me Your Spirit to live inside me. Let Emmanuel be more than a story to me—let it be my reality: God with me, forever. Thank You for filling me, for living in me, and for never leaving me. Seal this truth in my heart today. In Jesus' name. Amen.

God is not only with me — He lives in me by His Spirit. I will not be afraid.

Day 4: A World in Waiting

"The people walking in darkness have seen a great light." — Isaiah 9:2

B reathe in slowly... deep and full, like the first rays of morning stretching across a quiet valley. Hold it gently. Now breathe out, soft and steady, as if letting go of the long night.

Close your eyes. Imagine standing in the heart of a vast, shadowed world. The sky above is dark, an endless midnight, sprinkled with distant stars. They flicker like tiny lanterns, but they are not enough to chase away the heaviness of night. Feel it. A world waiting. A world in darkness. A world longing for something more.

Do you know what waiting feels like? It's like standing at the window on your birthday morning, watching for your friends to arrive, and every minute feels like an hour. Or like waiting for Christmas when the wrapped gifts are already under the tree — you see them, but you can't touch them yet. Or like waiting for summer break, when you know the rides and roller coasters are ahead, carrying you up and down in joy, but for now the days feel long and heavy. Waiting can feel discouraging. Sometimes lonely. Sometimes even frustrating.

That's what the world felt like before Jesus came. Generation after generation, people waited for God's promise. They hoped for the Messiah, the One who would bring peace, but the waiting stretched on so long that it felt like endless night. And any heart without Jesus still feels like that — alone in the dark, restless, longing for something more.

But then—far off at the horizon—a glow appears. At first it's faint, like a secret whispered on the wind. But slowly, steadily, the shimmer grows. Like dawn unfolding, like a flower opening its petals to the sun. Light begins to push back the night. Golden threads stretch across the sky. Hope glimmers again.

Pause. Breathe in the light. Let it touch your face. Let it sink into your chest. Let it fill your heart with quiet joy.

This light is Jesus. The Light of the World. The One every heart has been waiting for. Picture His light flowing like liquid gold, wrapping gently around you. It hums like a lullaby sung by the stars. With each breath, the shadows retreat, melting like mist before the rising sun.

You begin to walk. The path beneath your feet glows with dewy grass that sparkles like tiny diamonds. The air smells of rain-washed earth and blooming wildflowers. A chorus of life begins all around you — the rustle of leaves, the first calls of waking birds, the murmur of streams finding their voice. This is not just sunrise. This is new creation. God breathing His promise into the world: All things broken will be made whole again.

Now see a candle in your hand. Its flame dances strong and steady. You touch it to another, and then another, until the whole forest is alight with hundreds of flames, burning back the night. That is you. You carry His light inside you. It isn't meant to stay hidden. You are called to shine — bringing hope where there is sadness, joy where there is despair, peace where there is fear.

Pause here. Place your hand on your chest. Feel your heartbeat. Imagine the flame pulsing there, steady and true. Whisper this prayer: *Holy Spirit, shine the light of Jesus in me. Give me courage to follow Him and strength to share His love.*

Breathe in the light... Breathe out the shadows.

But think for a moment... what about those who are still waiting? The friends at school who don't know Jesus yet. The siblings who sometimes feel lonely or afraid. The people around you who still walk in darkness because they don't yet carry His light in their hearts. How will they see unless someone shows them? How will they feel the warmth unless someone shares it?

You are that someone. You carry His flame now — not to keep hidden, but to pass on. You don't have to be afraid or perfect. Even a small light can change the darkest room. So ask yourself quietly: *Who around me needs the light of Jesus? Who can I shine His hope to today?*

Yesterday, you discovered Emmanuel—God with us—not only in Bethlehem, but alive in you through His Spirit.

Today, you've seen how dark the world can be without Him. Yet even in the shadows, you carry His light — and with every step, that light grows brighter. Each breath brings you nearer to Bethlehem, nearer to the One who is the Light of the World.

Father God, thank You for sending Jesus, the Light who came into a world full of shadows. Help me never to keep this light to myself. Show me who around me needs hope and love, and give me courage to shine brightly for You. Step by step, as I walk toward the manger, let my life point others to Christ, the true Light of the world. Thank You for shining into my heart through Him, chasing away the darkness, and filling me with Your Spirit. In Jesus' name. Amen.

I am a shining light. I carry Jesus' hope and love into the world.

Day 5: The Word of the Lord Stands

"The grass withers, the flower fades, but the word of our God stands forever." — Isaiah 40:8

*F*ind a cozy spot where you can rest. Close your eyes softly, like a butterfly folding its wings. Take a slow, deep breath — fill your lungs like a big balloon. Hold it... now breathe out softly, like a calm breeze floating over a still lake.

Now, imagine a vast meadow stretching as far as your eyes can see. The air is fresh and sweet with the scent of wildflowers. The sun hangs low in the sky, painting golden shadows across the gentle hills. Look carefully. See the tall grass bending in the wind like waves upon the sea. Notice the flowers — bright reds, yellows, blues — each one delicate and full of life.

But then a gentle wind sweeps through the meadow. The grass sways. The flowers bow their heads. Petals begin to flutter away. Slowly, their colors fade. They curl soft and fragile, like they are saying goodbye to the warm sun. This is how so many things in life are — beautiful, but temporary. Like a flower blooming one day and wilting the next. Seasons come and go. Fun days end. Feelings change. Even things we treasure sometimes slip away.

Have you ever felt that? A favorite moment ending. A joyful day closing. The ride at the park stopping while you wished it could keep going. Waiting for something new to begin, only to feel the sadness of what has already passed.

But now, lift your eyes beyond the fading flowers. There at the edge of the meadow stands a tree — tall, steady, strong. Its roots sink deep into the ground, unshaken by the wind. Its branches stretch wide, full of green leaves that never wither, always alive. This tree is different. It does not fade. It does not fall. It stands through storm and sun. It holds firm against every season. This tree is like God's Word — steady, sure, and everlasting.

Now, imagine a glowing scroll floating before you. It is wrapped in golden light, alive with power and life. Slowly, it unfurls, and the words upon it glow with warmth. These words are not just ink on a page — they are alive, speaking directly to your heart. Feel them surround you like a soft blanket, comforting and protecting. Hear them wash over you like a gentle river flowing through a valley, washing away your fears and doubts.

Whisper softly: *God's Word is alive in me, shining bright and strong.*

But here's the secret: God's Word isn't just for one moment. Like water feeding a tree's roots, it must fill your heart every day. **Maybe you can already read the Bible on your own. Or maybe not yet — and that's okay. If you cannot, ask your mom or dad, or even an older brother**

or sister, to read it with you. Every time they read God's Word over you, it's like drops of living water sinking into your soul, making you steady, strong, and full of life.

Because when sadness comes... when a friend hurts your feelings... when you don't understand what's happening... His Word will be your safe place. Like a tower you can run into, and you will be safe.

Take a deep breath. Let your heart whisper: *I trust Your promises, Jesus. You are the Living Word in my heart forever.*

And remember—you are still on the road to the manger. Each day, step by step, you are drawing closer.

Yesterday, you carried His light into the shadows, and even there it could not be overcome.

Today, you've discovered that even in the waiting, God's Word never failed. And when the time was right, the Word became flesh and was born in Bethlehem. Every step you take reminds you that the Word who stood through generations is the same Word who became a baby wrapped in cloths, lying in a manger—Jesus, the Living Word.

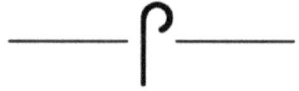

Heavenly Father, thank You for Your Word that never fades or fails. Help me to treasure Your Word every day. Remind me to read it, and when I ask my parents to read it with me, give them a willing heart to share it joyfully. Let my heart grow strong and steady like a tree planted deep in the ground. As I journey closer to the manger, let Your Word be my safe tower, my anchor, and my guide. Thank You that in a world where so many things change and pass away, Your promises remain steady and true. In Jesus' name. Amen.

God's Word is my safe place. His promises never fade, and His truth will guide me forever.

Day 6: Preparing the Way

"I will send my messenger, who will prepare the way before me." — Malachi 3:1

*F*ind a quiet, peaceful place where you can settle comfortably. If you want, gently close your eyes—or simply let your heart imagine. Take a deep, slow breath in—feel your lungs fill like a soft balloon rising into the sky. Hold... then breathe out slowly, like a gentle breeze blowing across a calm lake.

Picture yourself at the entrance of a wide, quiet path. The ground is soft beneath your feet, cushioned with moss and fallen leaves. Around you, tall trees stretch toward the sky, their branches swaying like arms lifted in prayer. The air is cool, fresh, and sweet with the smell of earth after rain. Take a few slow steps forward. Listen. The path whispers with peace. The birds sing encouragement in the branches overhead. A gentle breeze brushes your cheeks, carrying scents of wildflowers and whispers of promise. This path is like your heart. And because Jesus already lives inside you, God is gently tending it—making space for His voice to grow clearer in you, His love stronger in you.

Look closely. Do you remember what we said yesterday — to ask your parents or an older brother or sister to read God's Word with you? That wasn't just a small idea. It's because His Word is alive. When it enters your heart, it becomes like God's own hands. Stones of fear, doubt, and worry are lifted and rolled aside. Thorny vines of unkindness or pride are cut back carefully, making space for light. You feel His kindness in every touch—patient, gentle, steady. Now watch as He scatters seeds along the cleared earth. Seeds of joy, kindness, patience, love. Each seed glows softly with promise. Slowly, green shoots push up from the soil. You pause to watch the miracle—tender leaves unfolding toward the sun, tiny roots sinking deeper and deeper. This is what God is doing inside you: not planting Jesus again—for He already dwells in you—but nourishing what He planted, helping His life grow stronger in your heart each day.

Breathe slowly and whisper: Thank You, Lord, for living in my heart. Help me grow in Your love and grace.

Now listen. A voice echoes far away, steady and strong, as though carried on the wind: "*Prepare the way of the Lord... make His paths straight.*" Long ago, before Jesus was born in Bethlehem, God sent John the Baptist to be that voice. He called out to the people, urging them to turn from sin, to open their hearts, to be ready for the Messiah. John was like a gardener clearing weeds, like a builder smoothing the road—helping hearts become ready for Jesus to enter. And just as it was then, so it is now. Many hearts in our world are still unprepared. Some people do not yet know Jesus. Their paths are cluttered with stones of unbelief, overgrown with thorns of anger or fear. They are still waiting in the wilderness of darkness.

But here is the wonder: God not only prepares your heart—He also wants to use you to help prepare others. Every time you show kindness instead of anger, it is like rolling a stone from someone else's path. Every time you forgive, it is like pulling out a thorn. Every time you share Jesus' love, it is like planting a seed in someone's heart that can grow toward Him.

Take another breath. Place your hand on your heart and whisper: Thank You, Lord, for being in me. Help me prepare others to welcome You too.

Pause now and look ahead down the garden path. Far in the distance, beyond the trees, a soft glow shimmers—golden and warm, like lamplight in the night. With every step, it grows brighter, and you realize: this path is leading all the way to the manger. And with every stone God clears away, with every seed He plants and grows, with every kind word or act of love you share, you are moving closer. Each day uncovers more of the mystery waiting to be revealed—the Savior, born for you, resting in Bethlehem's cradle.

Yesterday, you discovered that though everything else fades, God's Word never fails.

Today, you see Him preparing your heart like a garden path, and through you, preparing others as well. Step by step, the way grows clearer, leading closer to the manger.

My Father, thank You for preparing my heart like a garden path. Thank You for clearing away doubts and fears, for planting seeds of Your love, and for helping them grow strong inside me. Now help me to help others—my friends, my family, and those who do not yet know You—so their hearts may be ready to welcome Jesus too. As I walk this path from the garden to the manger, keep me close to You, step by step, until I see Your glory more clearly. Thank You that through Christ You already live in me. In Jesus' name. A men.

Jesus lives in my heart, and as I walk the garden path to the manger, God will use me to help others welcome Him too.

Day 7: Mary Says Yes — Helping Others Say Yes Too

"I am the Lord's servant," Mary answered. "May your word to me be fulfilled." — Luke 1:38

F *ind a quiet, comfortable place to sit or lie down. Close your eyes gently, like a flower folding its petals at night. Take a deep breath in—slow and full, as if filling up a bright balloon. Hold it... and then breathe out softly, like a warm breeze drifting across a calm lake.*

Imagine walking through a little village long ago. The sun shines softly on stone walls, and the air carries the smell of warm bread and fresh wildflowers. Children laugh, birds sing, neighbors greet one another with cheerful voices. Step inside a small, sunlit room. A young girl stands there quietly. Her name is Mary. She is ordinary, simple, and humble, but her heart glows with a brave light.

Suddenly, a radiant angel appears, and the room shines as though the morning sun has risen all at once. The angel's words fill the air: she will carry God's Son, the Savior of the world. Mary's heart beats fast with wonder. She doesn't know how this can happen, but she chooses to trust. She lifts her eyes and answers with courage: "*I am the Lord's servant. May Your word to me be fulfilled.*"

Mary's yes was not small. It was strong, brave, and full of faith. She didn't need to understand everything; she only needed to trust God's love.

Now imagine that same light shining inside your own heart—a steady glow because Jesus lives there. His light isn't meant to stay hidden. God wants it to shine for others, so they can see His love too. Think of two people you know—a friend, a family member, maybe someone at school—who haven't yet said yes to Jesus. Picture their hearts like closed doors, waiting for kindness and love to gently knock.

Imagine your smile, your patience, or a simple act of kindness as a soft light shining through their door. Can you see it? The warmth, the safety, the love that helps them open up?

Picture yourself as a lamp glowing in the dark, steady and gentle. Your faith and love guide your friend's steps, like a lantern showing the way. Imagine walking alongside them, encouraging them until they find courage to whisper their own yes to God.

Feel the joy when someone discovers Jesus' love for themselves. It's like watching a flower bloom in the sunshine, or seeing a spark catch fire and spread warmth around.

Take a slow breath in... let it out gently. Whisper in your heart: "Jesus, help me shine Your love so others can find You."

Feel His peace flowing through you like a quiet river, carrying away worry, filling you with joy and courage.

Lift your eyes toward the road again—our journey from the garden to the manger.

Yesterday, you saw God preparing your heart like a garden path, planting seeds of His love and making room for His Word to grow.

Today, you've seen Mary's yes. Each yes is like a stone lifted from the path, another thorn pulled away, another step closer to Bethlehem. Step by step, you are walking nearer to the manger, where Jesus waits.

My Heavenly Father, thank You for Mary's brave yes. Help me to trust You even when I don't understand everything, and to believe that Your plans for me are good. Shine Your light through my life, so that my words, my actions, and even my quiet kindness can help open the doors of other hearts. Make me brave to say yes to You each day, and use my yes to draw others closer to Jesus. Let Your love spread like a flame, from one heart to another, until the whole world glows with the light of Christ's coming. Thank You that through Mary's obedience, You sent Your light into the world. In Jesus' name. Amen.

I carry the light of Jesus in my heart. My yes to Him makes me brave. Through my life, others will see His love and find the courage to say yes too.

Day 8: Joseph's Dream

"Joseph... did what the angel of the Lord had commanded him." — Matthew 1:24

Take a deep breath in... and let it out slowly. Again, breathe in deeply, filling your chest like a balloon, and breathe out gently, letting all your thoughts quiet down. Rest here a moment, still and calm, ready to listen.

Imagine the quiet streets of a little village at night. The sky is dark and full of twinkling stars. The houses are simple, made of stone, and everything is hushed. Step into one of those houses and you'll find Joseph.

Joseph is a good man. He works hard with his hands, shaping wood into strong tables and doors. He is also kind and gentle. He had promised to marry Mary. He dreamed of a happy life with her.

But now Joseph is troubled. Mary is going to have a baby—and the baby is not his. He doesn't understand what has happened. His heart feels heavy, like carrying a basket filled with stones. He doesn't want Mary to be laughed at or hurt by others. So he thinks of quietly ending the promise of marriage, hoping to keep her safe from shame.

That night, as Joseph finally closes his eyes, something amazing happens. In a dream, a bright angel appears. The angel's presence fills the room with light and peace. His voice is gentle but strong:

"Joseph, son of David, do not be afraid to take Mary as your wife. The child inside her is from the Holy Spirit. She will give birth to a Son, and you shall call His name Jesus, for He will save His people from their sins."

Joseph listens carefully. The words wash over him like sunlight breaking through a cloudy sky. His heart, once heavy, begins to lift. The confusion softens, replaced with peace.

When Joseph wakes up, morning light streams through the window. The village stirs awake outside, but Joseph's heart is different now. He has heard God's plan. He knows what he must do. With quiet courage, Joseph chooses to trust. He will stand beside Mary. He will obey God.

Think about Joseph's choice. He didn't have all the answers. He didn't understand every detail. But when God spoke, Joseph trusted and obeyed.

What about you? Is there something in your life that feels confusing, or too big to understand? Maybe at school, with friends, or even at home? You don't need to have every answer. Like Joseph, you can trust God to guide you. His plans are always good.

Take a deep breath and whisper in your heart: "*Lord, I don't need to understand everything. I just need to trust You.*"

Yesterday, you stood with Mary as she said yes to God's plan. Today, you walk with Joseph as he chooses to trust and obey. Step by step, you are moving closer to Bethlehem—closer to the manger where God's promise will be born.

Heavenly Father, thank You for Joseph's courage. Thank You that even when he was confused, he chose to trust and obey You. Help me to follow You too, even when I don't understand everything. Fill my heart with peace and courage, so I can walk each day in the plan You have made for me. I praise You, because Your ways are always good. In Jesus' name. Amen.

I will trust God's plan, even when I don't understand it.

Day 9: The Road to Bethlehem

"And Joseph also went up from Galilee, out of the city of Nazareth, into Judaea, unto the city of David, which is called Bethlehem; (because he was of the house and lineage of David:) To be taxed with Mary his espoused wife, being great with child."—Luke 2:4–5

Take a slow breath with me. Inhale deeply, filling your lungs with the cool morning air. Hold it gently for a count of three, then exhale fully, releasing the weight you've been carrying. Feel your body soften into stillness, your mind steadying like calm water at dawn.

Now, imagine the road before you—long, dusty, and winding beneath a sky washed in soft apricot and rose. The air is cool, scented with crushed herbs and the faint smoke of morning fires. Dust swirls like scattered gold at your feet as the sun's first rays climb the hills.

Walk beside Joseph and Mary. Mary's steps are slower now, her time is near. Some imagine her riding on a donkey, Joseph steady at her side. Others picture her walking, leaning on his arm. However it was, we know this: they kept moving forward together. Joseph's heart was steady, though questions pressed hard against him. Mary carried the Child promised by God, and each step was heavy with both weight and wonder.

They could have stayed behind. They could have said, "Mary is too close to giving birth—it's not safe to travel." But instead, they obeyed the command to go to Bethlehem. Obedience was their choice, even when it was hard. Obedience was their way of saying, "God, we trust You."

They did not choose this journey for comfort. Caesar had ordered every family to return to their hometown for a census. Mary was almost ready to give birth. They could have found excuses to stay behind, but they didn't. They obeyed. They trusted. Even though they didn't know what would happen in Bethlehem, they walked forward, step by step, into the unknown.

Sometimes you may not understand why you're told to do something—whether it's your parents asking you to help, your teacher setting rules in class, or your older sibling reminding you of what's right. You might not see the whole reason. But obedience is good. It keeps you safe. It honors those God placed over you. And most of all, it honors God Himself.

Think about this: Joseph and Mary didn't know what the next day would hold. They had no guarantee of where they would stay or how things would unfold. Yet they took the road because they believed God would be with them.

You may face roads like this, too. A move to a new school. Meeting new classmates. Starting something you've never tried before. It can feel scary not to know what's ahead. But just as God walked with Joseph and Mary, He walks with you. You can obey with a willing heart, and you can step forward with courage, trusting Him to guide every step. And so, as Joseph and Mary walked into the unknown, their obedience became courage. They trusted that God was already ahead of them, weaving His plan through every step of the journey.

Pause and breathe with me: "Lord, carry me when I am weary." Exhale: "Give me strength for the road ahead."

The path stretches endlessly, but it is more than stone and dust—it is a ribbon woven by God Himself, carrying His promise forward. Every ache, every sigh, every faltering step is gathered into His greater plan.

See Bethlehem rising in the distance—stone houses clustered close, the scent of fresh bread wafting on the breeze, children's laughter carried faintly through the air. Mary slows, her time drawing near. Joseph's hand rests at her back, steady and strong. The road has led to this place, where heaven's gift will be laid upon earth.

Take one last deep breath: "I will trust Your plan, even when the road is hard." Exhale: "I will obey and walk forward with courage, wrapped in Your love."

Yesterday, you saw Joseph's trust and obedience, even when he didn't understand everything.

Today, you see how obedience carried both Joseph and Mary forward into the unknown. They didn't wait for everything to be easy. They didn't demand to know the ending before they began the journey. They simply obeyed, and in that obedience, courage was born.

Your roads may feel uncertain too, but when you obey the right voices in your life—your parents, teachers, leaders, and above all God—you will discover that courage always walks beside you. And just like Joseph and Mary, every faithful step you take becomes part of God's story unfolding in you.

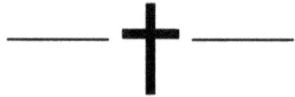

My Father, I thank You for walking with me on every road. Help me to obey those You have placed in my life and to honor You with my choices. Give me courage to walk into the unknown, trusting that You are already there, preparing the way. I praise You for being my strength when I feel weak and my guide when I cannot see what lies ahead. In Jesus' name. Amen.

I will obey with a willing heart, and I will walk forward with courage, knowing God is with me every step.

Day 10: The Heavy Journey

"He went there to register with Mary, who was pledged to be married to him and was expecting a child." — Luke 2:5

*T*ake a slow, deep breath in... let it feel like you're filling your lungs with cool, clean air under a night sky full of stars. Hold it gently... then breathe out, letting your shoulders drop and your heart grow calm.

The road is rough and dusty, and the hills keep rising. When Mary pauses to rest, Joseph waits with her, steady and strong, then together they walk on toward Bethlehem.

The sun has set, and the air grows cooler, yet the path is rough. Every bump, every stone, every turn feels heavier than the last. They do not complain. They just keep moving forward—step by step, mile by mile—because they know God is with them.

Close your eyes and feel it—the weight of the journey, the ache of tired feet, the longing for rest. Have you ever had a day like that? A day where everything feels heavy, and you wish you could stop, but you must keep going?

Take another breath in... and picture Jesus walking beside you on your own road. His steps match yours, His presence steady, His voice gentle: "I am with you. Keep going. You are not alone."

When school feels long and tiring... when friends leave you out... when family doesn't understand... when the road ahead feels too much—remember Mary and Joseph's journey. It was heavy, but God carried them through. And Jesus does the same for you. He lifts your burdens, shares your steps, and whispers courage into your heart.

Pause now. Breathe in His strength... breathe out your worries. Whisper softly: *"Jesus, thank You for walking with me when the journey feels heavy."*

When someone you know is carrying something heavy—maybe a friend who's sad, or a classmate who feels left out—you can be like Joseph walking beside Mary. You don't have to fix everything; just walking with them, praying for them, or sharing a kind word can make their road feel lighter. God often sends His strength through the love we give. And as you help someone else keep going, you'll find your own steps grow steadier too.

Yesterday, you saw how obedience carried Joseph and Mary forward, and in that obedience courage was born. Today, the stones feel sharper, the road harder beneath your feet. Yet you keep walking, because every step brings you nearer to Bethlehem, nearer to the manger, nearer to the King.

Heavenly Father, thank You for sending Jesus to walk with me on every journey. Give me courage to keep going, step by step, and help me remember that through Him You are always beside me. When I feel weak, remind me that Your strength never fails. I praise You for being my guide and my help. In Jesus' name. Amen.

Even when the road feels heavy, Jesus walks with me. I will keep moving forward, step by step, with Him.

Day 11: The Time Has Come

"And so it was, that, while they were there, the days were accomplished that she should be delivered." — Luke 2:6

T ake a deep breath in... and let it out slowly. Can you feel the stillness of waiting?

Mary and Joseph waited. The whole world waited. Not just for a few days, but for hundreds of years. Prophets had spoken of a Savior who would come, yet for so long the heavens felt quiet. Did God forget? Hearts must have wondered. But then Luke tells us in simple words: *the time came.* God remembered. God kept His promise.

Think about waiting in your own life. Sometimes waiting is light—like counting down to your birthday. Other times it feels endless. Maybe you've stared at the classroom clock, waiting for recess. Or stood in line at the swings, watching each person take their turn. Maybe you've waited at the school doors, hoping the next car to pull up was the one you were waiting for.

And sometimes waiting presses heavier. Waiting for a friend to forgive you. Waiting for someone sick to get better. Waiting for home to feel calm again when things are stormy. Waiting can ache. It can whisper, *Did God forget me?*

But listen closely—God never forgets. Just as He didn't forget Mary. Just as He didn't forget Joseph. Just as He didn't forget the whole world. At the right moment, Jesus came. And at the right moment in your life, God will answer too. He is never late. He never overlooks you. He always remembers.

Picture a giant clock in the sky, its hands turning—tick, tick, tick—day after day, year after year. People wait, hope, pray. And then suddenly the clock stops. Heaven's voice declares: Now! And Jesus enters the world.

That same God who said *Now* to the world will one day say *Now* to you. He knows exactly when the time is right.

Take a slow breath in... and whisper as you exhale: "*God always remembers me.*"

Yesterday, you felt the heaviness of the road beneath your feet. Today, you sense the weight of waiting—long years of hope pressing on your shoulders. But as you look ahead, you see Bethlehem glowing faintly in the distance. The waiting is almost over. The world's 'not yet' is turning into now.

Father Lord, thank You that You always keep Your promises. When I feel like giving up, remind me that You are never late and never forget me. Give me strength to wait and to hope in You. Thank You for being faithful to every promise You have spoken. All glory belongs to You. In Jesus' name. Amen.

God has not forgotten me. His timing is always perfect. I will trust Him while I wait.

Day 12: Shepherds in the Dark

"And there were in the same country shepherds abiding in the field, keeping watch over their flock by night." — Luke 2:8

*B*reathe in slowly, and as you do, feel the cool night air swirling gently around you, soft as a breeze through tall grass. Close your eyes and let your body rest, as though you are lying on a bed of moss beneath a vast, starry sky.

The field stretches wide around you, hills rising and falling like dark waves. Above, the sky is endless, scattered with sparkling stars. Beneath your feet the earth is cool, damp with dew. Nearby, sheep huddle together, their breathing steady, soft as a lullaby. You pull your cloak close, guarding against the chill, eyes scanning the horizon. It is quiet. It is still. You breathe in that stillness and whisper, "Lord, be my strength and calm in the night."

Suddenly, the quiet is broken. Light pours down from heaven, brighter than fire, warmer than the sun. It spills across the hills, wrapping the sheep, the grass, the very air in a golden glow. You lift your arm to shield your eyes, but you cannot look away. Darkness has fled; holiness stands before you.

An angel steps forward, radiant and strong, his face shining like dawn. His voice rings clear, steady as a bell: "Do not be afraid. I bring you good tidings of great joy, which shall be to all people. For unto you is born this day in the city of David a Saviour, which is Christ the Lord."

The words fall over you like a blanket of peace. This message is not spoken in a palace, not delivered to kings—it is spoken here, in the quiet fields, to shepherds in the dark.

To you. To me. God's glory reaching into ordinary places, ordinary hearts.

And just like God came to the shepherds in their ordinary field, He has already come to you. Do you remember when you said yes to Jesus in **Day 2**? Do you remember when you opened the door wide for the Holy Spirit in **Day 3**? That was when His light filled you. You don't have to wait for Him to find you—He is already with you, every single day.

So when homework feels too hard... when a friend hurts your feelings... when you lie awake at night and the room feels dark... remember: Jesus is with you in that very moment, steady and strong, filling your heart with His peace.

And just like the shepherds couldn't keep the good news to themselves, you can carry His light too. A kind word, a smile, a helping hand—these are ways His light shines through you into the lives of others.

Whisper softly: "*Thank You, Lord, for shining Your light in my life, every day.*"

For a moment the field is quiet again, as if creation itself has heard your prayer. The sheep stir but do not scatter; they seem wrapped in the same peace that covers you. Slowly the glow folds back into the heavens, and the stars return, steady and watchful. The night is no longer the same. Darkness still lingers, but now it carries a promise—something holy, something new.

You watch the shepherds rise, their faces lit with awe. They look at one another, breathless. What would you do? Stay in the field, or run to see the Savior the angel spoke of?

The shepherds choose. They leave their flocks in God's care and set out toward Bethlehem. From where you stand, you can almost see the faint glow ahead—the stable where hope rests. But not yet. For now, you walk in wonder, following the promise spoken in the night.

Yesterday, you carried the weight of waiting, but you also learned that God never forgets His promise. Today, you watch shepherds rise from the fields, leaving their flocks in God's care to follow the promise spoken to them. Step by step, you walk beneath the stars, closer to the manger where hope has come at last.

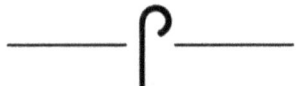

Dear God, thank You for shining Your light into my darkness. When I feel small or hidden, remind me that You see me and that You are already with me. Fill me with Your hope, and let me carry Your light into the world around me.

Thank You for choosing the ordinary places of life to show Your glory. All praise belongs to You. In Jesus' name. Amen.

I opened my heart wide to You, Lord, and Your Spirit lives in me. I carry Your light—gently, boldly, faithfully—through every ordinary step of my day.

Day 13: Glory in the Sky

"Glory to God in the highest, and on earth peace, good will toward men." — Luke 2:14

T *ake a slow breath in... and let it out.* The night is quiet, the air cool, the field wide and dark. For a moment, all you hear is the soft shuffle of sheep, the gentle sigh of the wind, and your own steady heartbeat.

You tilt your head back to look at the stars. They twinkle like tiny lamps hung high above, far away, silent and small. The world feels still. Almost too still.

And then—it happens. The sky tears open like a curtain pulled wide, and light floods in, brighter than fire, brighter than the sun at noon. It pours over the hills, spilling across the fields like a golden river. Every blade of grass shimmers. Every stone glows. The dark night is gone, swallowed up in glory.

You can feel the light on your face, warm and strong, like standing close to a blazing fire. Your chest rises faster, your eyes stretch wide, your heart pounds so hard you can almost hear it in your ears.

Then the sound begins. At first, one voice—loud, clear, filling the sky. But before you can even breathe, thousands more rush in. The whole sky is alive with song. Angels. Everywhere. Too many to count. From one end of the horizon to the other, the heavens are filled with shining messengers of light.

Their voices roll over the fields like thunder wrapped in music, like a waterfall crashing but turning into song as it falls: "*Glory to God in the highest, and on earth peace, good will toward men!*"

The sound is so strong it shakes the ground beneath your feet. The hills echo with it. The sheep stand frozen in stillness, wide-eyed, glowing in the light.

You look at the shepherds beside you. Some drop to their knees, covering their faces with trembling hands. Some lift their arms high, as if they could catch the music in their palms. Some laugh through tears, too overwhelmed to hold it in. And you—what would you do? Would you fall on your knees too? Would you close your eyes and let the sound wash over you? Or would you stand frozen, unable to look away from the glory filling the sky?

Take a deep breath in... and whisper with awe: "*Thank You, Lord, for filling the night with Your glory.*"

The song rises higher, voices weaving together in perfect harmony, soaring like rivers of light across the heavens. Wings shimmer and flash like silver flames. The angels move like waves of fire and wind, and still they sing: *Glory... glory... glory...*

It feels endless. Eternal. Like the sky itself will never stop praising.

And the peace they sing about isn't just for shepherds in a field long ago. It is for you. When homework feels heavy, when brothers or sisters argue, when your heart feels restless or afraid — remember this: Jesus was born to bring you His peace. A peace that calms storms inside, a peace that helps you forgive, a peace that grows like fruit in your heart through the Holy Spirit. And just as the shepherds carried the good news, you can carry His peace too—into your classroom, your family, your friendships—with kind words and gentle choices.

As you think about that peace, you glance again at the field. The glow still lingers, shimmering around you, wrapping both you and the shepherds in quiet wonder.

And then, slowly, it begins to fade. The light folds back into the heavens. The voices grow softer, like the last notes of a lullaby drifting away. The stars return, sparkling in their quiet places. The night grows still again—but not the same stillness as before. This stillness hums with promise. It hums with peace.

The shepherds breathe hard, their eyes wide and shining. They look at one another, trembling—not in fear, but in awe. Their hearts burn with holy fire. And then their feet begin to move. They cannot stay here. They must go.

And step by step, you go too—closer to Bethlehem, carrying the sound of heaven's song in your heart.

Yesterday, you watched the shepherds rise, leaving their sheep in God's care to follow the promise. Today, the whole sky opened with glory, and you heard the angels' voices fill the night with praise and peace. Step by step, you carry that song with you, leading you closer to Bethlehem—closer to the manger where Jesus waits.

Heavenly Father, thank You for filling the night with Your glory. Let the song of heaven live inside my heart today, and help me shine that peace into the lives around me. Thank You for sending angels to sing of joy and peace, reminding the world that Your promises are true. All praise belongs to You. In Jesus' name. Amen.

Your glory fills my night, Lord. Your peace and joy guide every step I take.

Day 14: A Sign You Can Hold

"This will be a sign to you: You will find a baby wrapped in cloths and lying in a manger." — Luke 2:12

*T*ake a deep, slow breath in... and let it out.

The night around you feels different now. The fields are the same, the stars are the same, but they seem to shine with a new kind of light. The echo of the angels' song is still in the air, like the last notes of music that refuse to fade. You can almost hear it still ringing in your ears: *Glory to God in the highest... peace on earth...*

And then, the words of the angel return to you — not just the announcement of a Savior, but something even more personal, something you can look for with your own eyes: *"This will be a sign to you: You will find a baby wrapped in cloths and lying in a manger."*

You whisper those words again and again, almost tasting their wonder. A baby. Wrapped in cloths. Lying in a manger. What kind of sign is this? Would you expect God's great promise to look so small? Would you think His gift would be placed not in a palace but in an animal's feeding trough?

Close your eyes and let your imagination rise. What will it be like when you see Him? Will His tiny fingers curl around a shepherd's hand? Will His newborn cry echo softly in the night, fragile yet filled with life? Will His eyes, when they open, reflect the very light of heaven?

This is no crown you must admire from far away. No throne you are too small to approach. No wall to keep you out. This is a sign you can kneel beside, a sign you could almost hold.

Whisper quietly: *"Thank You, Lord, for giving a sign I can draw close to, a sign I can treasure in my heart."*

The shepherds are restless now. Their feet shift on the ground, their eyes shining with urgency. They know what they must look for. They know who they are searching for. Their hearts burn with eagerness, and yours does too.

You don't see the baby yet — not tonight, not now — but you walk with hope alive inside you. Every step you take carries the words like a lamp lighting the way: *"You will find a baby... wrapped in cloths... lying in a manger."* And you realize: *This is how I walk in real life too — carrying God's promises in my heart, even before I see them with my eyes.*

The journey continues. The promise is ahead. And with every breath, you are moving closer to the sign God has given.

Yesterday, the heavens opened wide with a song of glory and peace. Today, you hear the angel's promise of a sign — not a throne or a crown, but a baby wrapped in cloths, lying in a manger. Step by step, you follow the shepherds, your heart filled with wonder and questions, eager to see the promise with your own eyes.

My Father, I praise You for giving a sign that invites me to draw near. Thank You for coming in a way I can imagine holding close—small enough for my heart to understand, yet great enough to change the whole world. Keep my heart soft with wonder and steady with expectation as I walk toward You. When waiting feels long, remind me that Your promises are sure, and that every step with You brings me closer to hope fulfilled. All glory belongs to You forever. In Jesus' name. Amen.

Your promise stirs my wonder, Lord. Each step takes me nearer to the sign of Your love.

Day 15: Jesus, the Name Above All

"You shall call His name Jesus, for He shall save His people from their sins." — Matthew 1:21

B *reathe in deeply, filling your lungs with the cool night air. Let it out slowly, like a sigh of rest. The world around you is wrapped in stillness, as if the stars themselves are holding their breath. Feel the quiet cover you like a soft blanket, warm and safe, holding you close.*

Now picture a small wooden workshop, lit by a flickering lamp. The smell of fresh-cut wood lingers in the air, and the shadows of tools dance gently on the walls. Joseph is there, working with steady hands, yet inside his heart is heavy with questions. How can he care for this child? How can he, an ordinary man, protect the Son of God?

Then the silence shifts. A voice comes, soft but strong, tender yet full of power: "*You shall call His name Jesus, for He shall save His people from their sins.*"

Joseph's breath catches. His heart beats like a steady drum, echoing deep inside him. That name—Jesus—is more than a word. It is a promise. It is rescue. It is hope.

Say His name softly now: Jesus.

What does it feel like to whisper it? Does it feel like light breaking into the dark? A gentle hand reaching for yours when you are afraid? A song that fills your heart, even when the night is quiet?

Joseph did not understand everything yet. He still wondered. He still asked. But the name Jesus rested inside him like an anchor, pulling his heart toward trust. And that same name rests inside you.

This is more than imagination. When you're afraid at night, whisper His name. When unkind words try to press you down, let His name lift you up. When you feel small, remember His name is big enough to cover you.

The name of Jesus is a crown, not of gold, but of kindness. It is a shield, not of iron, but of love. It is a song that will never fade, a promise that will never fail. His name is written on your heart like a banner that says: *I belong to Him.*

And you realize: *This is how I can live—not only whispering His name in quiet moments, but standing tall in real life, knowing I am safe, protected, and never forgotten.*

Take a deep breath, letting that name fill your whole being: Jesus.

Yesterday, you heard the angel's promise of a sign—a baby wrapped in cloths and lying in a manger. Today, you learn His name: Jesus, the Savior who rescues His people from their sins. Step by step, you carry that name in your heart, walking closer to Bethlehem, closer to the One whose name is above every name.

Father, I praise You because the name of Jesus is holy, strong, and full of life. Thank You that His name brings light in my darkness, peace in my fears, and hope when I wait. When I whisper the name of Jesus, remind me that You are near—steadying my heart, lifting my head, and calling me Your own. Let His name be on my lips in prayer, in worship, and in the way I live each day. May my words carry kindness, my steps carry courage, and my life reflect the power of His name. All glory belongs to You through Jesus, the name above all names. In Jesus' name. Amen.

Your name is my shelter and my song, Jesus. I will whisper it, trust it, and carry it forever.

Day 16: The Gift We Didn't Deserve

"For unto us a child is born, unto us a son is given..." — Isaiah 9:6

T ake a slow breath in... and let it out again. The night feels calm around you, like the hush that falls in a classroom when everyone is waiting to see who the teacher will call on next. The stars sparkle above like a hundred tiny lanterns, steady and bright.

Think for a moment about gifts. Sometimes we earn gifts as rewards, don't we? Maybe in school you've had a chart where you earn stickers for listening well, or points when you finish your work on time. Maybe you've been given a prize for sitting quietly, or a treat for helping out at home. Those gifts feel special, but they come because of what you've done.

But what about a gift you didn't earn? Imagine one day you're sitting at your desk, and the teacher suddenly walks over and places the biggest, shiniest prize in your hands. Not because you were quiet. Not because you got all the answers right. Not because you did anything to deserve it—but simply because the teacher loves you. Wouldn't that feel surprising? Almost unbelievable?

That is what God did for us. The Bible says, "For unto us a child is born, unto us a son is given." Not earned. Not bought. Not deserved. Given. Jesus was not a prize for the best-behaved or a reward for those who followed every rule perfectly. He was a gift for everyone—even when we were messy, even when we got it wrong, even though none of us could ever deserve Him.

Close your eyes and imagine holding a gift in your hands. It's not wrapped in glittering paper or tied with fancy ribbons. Instead, it's soft, wrapped in simple cloth, small enough to cradle gently. Inside is the greatest treasure the world has ever known—the Son of God, given for you, before you even knew to ask.

Whisper softly: Thank You, Lord, for giving me the gift I could never earn.

And you realize: This is how I can live when I feel undeserving—still holding on to Jesus as my treasure, because He was given to me anyway.

Joseph may have wondered too, standing beneath the stars, remembering the angel's words about this child's name: Jesus—the One who will save His people from their sins. How could one child be such a gift? How could one name carry so much hope? Yet Joseph knew this was not a gift for the few—it was a gift for all.

Take a deep breath now, and picture that gift glowing softly in your hands. It isn't loud or glittering, but it is steady and warm, like a flame that never fades. The more you hold it, the more you realize: this gift is not just for today—it is forever.

Whisper again: Jesus, You are my gift, my treasure, my hope.

And so you walk with the shepherds, step by step, hearts alive with wonder. You don't deserve this gift. None of us do. But it has been given anyway. Freely. Joyfully. Out of love too deep to measure. And each step toward Bethlehem is a reminder that the gift is real—and it is waiting.

Yesterday, you learned His name—Jesus, the One who saves His people from their sins. Today, you discover that He is the greatest gift, given not because we earned Him, but because God's love is bigger than anything we could deserve. Step by step, you walk with the shepherds, amazed at the gift of love that draws you closer to Bethlehem.

Father, I thank You for the gift of Jesus, the treasure I could never deserve. Your love reached me when I was weak, when I failed, and when I could give You nothing in return. Thank You that Your Son was given freely—not as a reward for the good, but as hope for all of us who need saving. When I feel unworthy, remind me that Jesus is still mine, and that Your love still covers me. Let this gift change the way I live—help me to share kindness freely, forgive quickly, and love deeply, just as You have loved me. All glory and thanks belong to You forever. In Jesus' name. Amen.

Jesus, You are the gift I could never earn. I will treasure You always and let Your love shine through me.

Day 17: Peace in Person

"Peace I leave with you, my peace I give unto you: not as the world giveth, give I unto you." — John 14:27

*T*ake *a deep breath in... and let it out slowly. Around you, the night stirs with sound, like a wild wind rushing through the trees, leaves twirling and tumbling in every direction. The noise seems everywhere at once, but as you close your eyes, you hear it begin to soften. The rushing wind becomes a gentle breeze. The chaos fades into a lullaby, quiet and calm, brushing against your skin like a tender hand.*

Now imagine a storm swirling inside your chest—a storm of worry, confusion, and racing thoughts. Thunder cracks like sharp words you've heard. Lightning flashes like sudden fears that startle you. The winds howl with every anxious thought that spins round and round in your mind. The storm feels too big for you to calm on your own.

But then—Jesus steps into the storm. Not with a sword or a shout, not with anger or force, but with hands stretched wide, gentle as a soft touch on your cheek. His presence does not push the storm away all at once, but suddenly the noise feels smaller because He is near.

His voice rises above the chaos—not loud, but steady and strong, like a slow drum beating in the middle of the storm: "Peace I leave with you; my peace I give to you."

The words settle into your heart like soft rain after a long, hot drought—soaking deep into the dry places, bringing quiet life where fear once lived. And you realize: *This is how His peace reaches me when my thoughts spin too fast.*

Picture that peace as a glowing ember inside your chest. It doesn't flicker when the winds blow. It doesn't vanish when the skies darken. It stays steady, warm, and bright—something you can always hold onto, no matter how wild the storm around you becomes.

Take another deep breath, slow and full. Hold it for a moment, then let it out like you're blowing dandelion seeds into the air, releasing your worries into the hands of Jesus.

Whisper softly: *Jesus, Your peace fills me with calm and courage.*

And you realize: *This calm I feel now is the same calm I can carry when my heart wants to panic or when the classroom feels too loud.*

Now imagine wrapping yourself in a soft, thick blanket, heavy with comfort, woven from silence and starlight. It doesn't stop the storm outside, but it holds you safe inside, warm and steady, as if you're being hugged by someone who loves you more than words can say.

Even when voices rise loud, even when worries swirl like leaves in the wind, Jesus' peace is like a rock beneath your feet—firm, unshaken, and strong enough to carry you through. And you realize: *This peace is not just in my imagination—it is how Jesus holds me steady when the world feels noisy and unsure.*

Breathe in calm... breathe out fear. Whisper again: *Jesus, Your peace is my shelter.*

Now picture yourself standing on the shore of a wide, peaceful lake. The water ripples gently, glowing silver under the moonlight. The waves lap quietly at the shore, never rushing, never roaring. This is the peace Jesus gives—a calm that doesn't come from everything being perfect, but from knowing that even when storms rise, He stands beside you and holds you steady.

Let that lake of peace fill your heart, washing away every noise, every worry, every fear—until only His quiet remains. And you realize: *This is the way I can live tomorrow, too—resting in His peace, no matter what comes.*

Take one last deep breath, hold it close like a treasure, and release it slowly.

Whisper: *Jesus, I rest in Your unshakable peace.*

Yesterday, you discovered that Jesus is the gift we didn't deserve—given freely out of love. Today, you learn that He is also peace itself, a peace the world cannot give. Step by step, you walk forward with the shepherds, carrying not only the promise of a gift but the quiet strength of peace that stays with you, even in life's storms.

Father, I praise You for giving us Jesus, my Prince of Peace. Thank You that no storm is stronger than His calm and no fear can rise higher than His love. When my heart feels restless, remind me through Him that You are near, steadying my steps and quieting my thoughts. Let the peace of Christ rest on me today, and may it overflow into gentle words, kind actions, and calm that others can feel. All glory belongs to You, through Jesus, my Prince of Peace. In Jesus' name I pray. Amen.

Jesus, You are my peace. No storm, no noise, no fear can shake me when You are near.

Day 18: Great Joy for All People — Living the Christmas Joy Today

"And the angel said unto them, Fear not: for, behold, I bring you good tidings of great joy, which shall be to all people." — Luke 2:10

*T*ake *a deep breath in... and let it out slowly. Around you the world feels busy and loud—like a classroom buzzing with voices, like shoes tapping all at once on the floor, like colors flashing so quickly you can hardly keep up. But then you close your eyes, and inside you, the noise begins to fade. The storm inside your heart quiets down, and you feel Jesus leaning close.*

Then you hear the angel's words, fresh and alive as if spoken right now: "Do *not be afraid. I bring you good news that will cause great joy for all the people.*" Not just happiness for a moment. Not just laughter that fades when the game ends. But joy. Deep, glowing joy that stays even when the night feels long.

Imagine that joy like a spark glowing inside your chest. At first it is small, but it grows brighter, stronger, warmer. It spreads through you like a lantern glowing in the dark, shining out into every corner of your heart. Then it bubbles over—like a fountain that won't stop flowing, like bubbles rising up and popping with laughter, like a song you can't help but sing.

And you realize: *This is how I can live even on hard days—holding joy inside me like a light that does not go out, because Jesus has given it to me.*

What does joy feel like to you? Is it a smile you can't hide? Is it laughter that makes your stomach hurt? Is it a warm light inside that keeps glowing even when you feel tired?

Whisper softly: *Jesus, thank You for joy that lights up even my darkest days.*

Now imagine that joy wrapping around you like a glowing cloak—soft, warm, and sparkling with kindness. But the cloak doesn't just stay with you. Its light stretches outward, reaching your family, your friends, even strangers who feel sad or forgotten. You see their faces brighten when joy touches them, like candles being lit one after another until the whole room glows.

How could you share that joy? Could you offer a smile to someone who looks lonely? Could you speak kind words when others are unkind? Could you share what you have—even something small—so another heart feels loved?

Picture the shepherds now. They are no longer just standing in the fields. Their eyes shine, their feet can hardly stay still. Some are laughing through tears, others are clapping each other on the back, all of them full of wonder. The angel's message has set their hearts on fire with joy, and they cannot keep it to themselves.

They hurry toward Bethlehem—not dragging their feet, but almost running, their voices bubbling over with excitement. And you walk with them. Every step you take feels lighter, brighter, filled with joy that doesn't belong to one person alone, but to all people everywhere.

Joy is not quiet like peace. Joy is alive, overflowing, moving from one heart to another. It is like sunshine bursting out after days of gray rain, like a campfire everyone gathers around for warmth, like music that makes your feet want to dance.

This is the joy Jesus brings—the joy of Christmas, the joy of knowing God has come close.

Take another deep breath now... breathe in His joy, hold it close... and breathe it out, letting it spill into the world around you.

Whisper: *Father, thank You for Jesus' joy in me. Help me share it wherever I go.*

Yesterday, you discovered that Jesus is peace itself—a calm the world cannot give, steady even in life's storms.

Today, you feel His joy—bright, bubbling, overflowing—a joy not just for you, but for all people. Step by step, you move with the shepherds, your heart bursting with good news, your steps lighter with the joy of Christmas drawing you nearer to Bethlehem.

Father, I thank You for sending Jesus to bring joy so big it fills my heart and cannot be contained. Thank You that this joy is not just for one person, but for the whole world. When I grow weary, let the joy of Christ be my strength; when I feel small, remind me through Him that I am loved. Help me carry this joy today—not only inside me, but outward through smiles, kindness, and words that lift others up. All glory to You, the Giver of true joy, through Jesus Christ my Lord. Amen.

Jesus, You are my joy and my song. Your joy shines in me, and I will share it wherever I go.

Day 19: A Savior, Not a Season

"For unto you is born this day in the city of David a Saviour, which is Christ the Lord."
— Luke 2:11

T*ake a deep breath in... and let it out slowly. The night is still and quiet, like the hush just before the sun rises. The sky begins to glow faintly with soft colors—pink, gold, and blue blending like gentle watercolor strokes. The town of Bethlehem still sleeps, its streets hushed, lanterns flickering in the windows of stone houses. You breathe in the crisp air, fresh and cool, as though the whole world is holding its breath, waiting.*

And then the angel's words echo again: "*Today in the city of David, a Savior has been born to you.*" This was no ordinary message. Not an announcement about decorations, not a call to prepare for parties or feasts, not even a holiday that would pass away. It was the news of a Savior—a Rescuer, a Friend, a King who came not just for one night, but for all time.

Imagine Bethlehem's alleys bathed in soft lamplight, the quiet murmur of animals in their stalls, the faint rustle of straw. Somewhere nearby lies the baby, wrapped in cloths, resting in a manger. The air smells of hay and wood, the quiet broken only by the soft breathing of His mother and the rustle of the stable. Small, ordinary details—but within them rests the greatest gift the world has ever known.

Breathe in the wonder... hold it gently... then breathe out slowly, letting awe fill your heart.

Whisper softly: *Jesus, You are the gift beyond all gifts, the love that never fades.*

Think of the things we often connect to Christmas—twinkling lights that shine bright for a season, presents wrapped in paper that is torn and thrown away, cookies baked and gone in a day. They are fun, warm, and beautiful, but they do not last. The angel's message was not about things that end. It was about someone who stays. A Savior who is not here for a moment, but forever.

Why would God send us a Savior instead of just giving us celebrations or decorations? What does it mean that He gave us His very Son, not for one day, but for every day of our lives?

Imagine reaching out to touch that love—real, steady, soft as a warm blanket on a cold night. Feel it wrap around your shoulders, not only for December, not only when life feels happy, but every single day, even in the hardest ones.

Whisper again: *Jesus, You are my Rescuer, my light, my forever Friend.*

The angel didn't say, "Enjoy this moment and move on." He said, "*Today in the city of David, a Savior has been born to you.*" That joy is not tied to one night. It is a joy that does not fade like snow melting under the sun. It is a joy that walks with you into January, February, March, and every day beyond.

Picture yourself holding that joy inside you like a glowing lantern. Its light never dims. Wherever you go, it shines—a steady flame reminding you that Jesus came for all seasons, all years, all moments.

Take another deep breath in... let it out... and whisper: Thank You, Jesus, for being my Savior not for a season, but forever.

Yesterday, you carried the joy of Christmas in your heart—a joy meant for all people. Today, you hear the angel's clear words: a Savior has been born to you. Step by step, you walk with the shepherds, remembering this is not just about one night or one season. It is about a Savior who came to stay—with you, always.

Father, I praise You for sending Jesus to be my Savior forever. Thank You that He is more than a holiday, more than a season, more than a moment in time. Your love through Him covers me in January and in June, in days of laughter and in days of tears. Keep my heart awake to Your presence beyond Christmas morning, and let my life shine with the hope of Christ wherever I go. All glory belongs to You, through Jesus, my Savior and my King. In His name I pray. Amen.

Jesus, You are my Savior forever— not just for a season, but for all my days.

Day 20: The Shepherd Who Became a Lamb

"Behold the Lamb of God, which taketh away the sin of the world." — John 1:29

T ake a slow, deep breath in... let it out gently. The air is cool and fresh, like standing in a meadow at sunrise. The grass glistens with dew, and sheep graze quietly, their soft bleating rising and falling like a lullaby. Somewhere close by stands the Shepherd—watchful, strong, His voice steady and kind. He knows every sheep by name, and they follow Him with trust because He has never failed to care for them.

Now listen—across the field, another voice rings out. It is John the Baptist, his words like a trumpet in the still morning: "Behold, the Lamb of God, which taketh away the sin of the world!" The words echo, bouncing off the hills. The shepherds glance up. You look too. Who could this Lamb be?

Pause for a moment. Think of what a shepherd does: he leads, protects, guards from wolves, finds safe paths, and feeds his sheep. A shepherd gives strength. Now think of a lamb: small, gentle, without defense, carried easily in arms. In Bible times, lambs were offered to God, pure and spotless, to say, "Please forgive us." The shepherd is the strong one who saves; the lamb is the one given up. Two very different roles.

But here is the wonder: Jesus, the Good Shepherd who knows and guards His sheep, chose to also become the Lamb. The Shepherd became the Lamb—strong becoming weak, leader becoming the one laid down. Imagine it: the teacher stepping into the student's desk to take the failing grade. The older brother stepping forward to take the punishment so the younger can go free. The captain of the team sitting on the bench so another player can shine. That is what Jesus did—He took our place.

Breathe in deeply, feel the weight of that love... breathe out slowly, letting gratitude fill your chest.

Whisper softly: *Jesus, You are my Shepherd, and You became the Lamb for me.*

Picture it now. The Shepherd lifts a lamb into His arms—its wool soft, its heartbeat small and steady. He carries it through valleys and shadows, protecting it from danger. That lamb is safe. But then, in a mystery of love, the Shepherd says, "*I will be the Lamb in your place.*" He lays Himself down so the flock can live free, whole, forgiven. The One who carried became the One carried away.

Think for a moment about what that means for you. Every wrong thing you've done, every mistake, every heavy weight—Jesus carried it as the Lamb. The Shepherd did not just guide you; He rescued you by becoming the gift no one deserved but everyone needed. His love is soft as wool and strong as the sunrise.

Take another deep breath. Hold it gently. Then let it out, like letting go of every fear and guilt you've ever held.

Whisper again: *Jesus, I trust You as my Shepherd, and I thank You as my Lamb.*

Yesterday, you remembered that Jesus is a Savior not just for a season but for every day. Today, you walk another step with the shepherds, seeing the wonder: the Shepherd Himself became the Lamb, trading His strength for your weakness so you could be free.

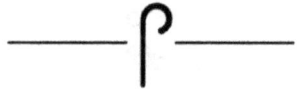

Father, I praise You for giving us Jesus, both Shepherd and Lamb. Thank You that through Him You lead me with strength and show love by laying down His life. When I wander, call me back to Your voice; when I feel weighed down, remind me that He has carried it all. Keep me close to Your side, safe in the grace You gave so freely through Him. All thanks and glory belong to You. In Jesus' name. A men.

Jesus, my Shepherd and my Lamb—You carried my sin and gave Yourself for me. I will follow Your voice and rest in Your love.

Day 21:
The Presence
That Changes
Everything

"The Word became flesh, and dwelt among us." — John 1:14

C lose your eyes gently. Take a deep, slow breath—like you're drawing in the fresh air of a brand-new morning. Smell the sweetness of flowers opening, feel the coolness of the air brushing your skin, notice how even the silence feels alive. Exhale slowly, and let your heart grow calm. You are ready to welcome a Presence that is not far, not hidden, but near.

Picture Jesus—the Word. Not just words on a page, but the living Word of God Himself. From the very beginning, Jesus was there. When God said, "Let there be light," it was His Word—Jesus—that shone out and made it happen. Everything God spoke came alive through Him.

Imagine that very first sunrise pouring color into the world—the dark sky suddenly glowing with gold because of Jesus. His light chased away the shadows then, and He still does the same today. When your heart feels dark, He shines His light inside you, warm and bright. Breathe in: Jesus, You are my light. Breathe out: You chase away my darkness.

See the world springing to life—green grass bursting from the ground, birds spreading their wings and singing, oceans filling with fish that leap and dance. Every heartbeat, every breath, every flower and star came alive through Him. And just as He gave life to creation, He gives life to you—life that fills your spirit with joy. Whisper: Jesus, You are my life.

And why did He do it? Because of love. Before you were born, Jesus already knew your name. When God spoke the world into being, love was woven into every part of it. Imagine Him threading His love into the stars, into the oceans, into the very air you breathe. That same love wraps around you now and will never let go. *Say softly: Jesus, You are love. And You love me.*

Pause here. Let the wonder settle in your heart. The same Jesus who was at creation—the One who is light, life, and love—chose to come close. He wrapped Himself in skin, soft and small, like any baby. Hands that could hold you. A voice that could laugh with you. Feet that could walk dusty roads. He became someone you could see, hear, touch, and follow. *Whisper with me now: "Jesus, Your presence fills my heart with peace."*

When Jesus is near, fear shrinks down like a shadow that can't reach you. Worry unravels like knots being untied. Joy blooms inside you, surprising and unstoppable, like wildflowers after a spring rain. And love—oh, love stretches wide—like a giant oak tree, arms reaching out to cover and embrace everyone around you. His presence is not a quick flash of light that fades. It is steady. Strong. Always here.

Yesterday, you saw the wonder of the Shepherd who became the Lamb, trading His strength for your weakness so you could be free.

Today, the garden around you grows quieter, as if all creation is hushed in waiting. Even the stars lean close, shining with the light that has always been His. You keep walking, your heart stirring with wonder. The Word who was light, life, and love is drawing near... yet still hidden.

Father, thank You for sending Jesus to come near. Thank You that He chose to live among us—not far, but close enough to touch, to hear, to follow. Fill me today with wonder, with joy, and with peace that only You can give through Him. Thank You that Your love never changes and Your presence never leaves. In Jesus' name. Amen.

The Word became flesh and made His home among us. His presence changes everything—I am never alone.

Day 22: The Birth of Jesus

"While they were there, the time came for the baby to be born, and she gave birth to her firstborn, a son. She wrapped him in cloths and placed him in a manger, because there was no guest room available for them." — Luke 2:6-7

F eel the heavy hush of night wrapping softly around you like a warm blanket—quiet, yet alive with the soft sounds of a sleeping world. Close your eyes, take a slow breath, and breathe in the cool air, scented with earth, hay, and the faint sweetness of wildflowers resting under the stars. Let your heart rest in the stillness, safe and sheltered.

Picture Bethlehem—its narrow stone streets bathed in moonlight, quiet except for the distant murmur of voices and the shuffle of animals in their stalls. Golden patches of lamplight spill across rough walls, but most of the town is asleep.

At the edge of this town, in a small, simple shelter, a miracle unfolds. Mary's breath is heavy but steady, her face glowing with both pain and hope. Joseph keeps watch, whispering silent prayers, his heart racing with awe. Heaven's promise is about to arrive.

And then—it happens. Not with thunder or trumpets, but with the tiniest sound: the cry of a newborn baby. The King of Heaven has entered the world quietly, clothed in fragile humanity. Mary holds Him close, wrapping Him in cloths. The place is humble, the night is ordinary, yet holiness fills the air like a fragrance too strong to hide.

Jesus came in silence. No drums, no crowds, no fireworks—only the quiet cry of a baby. God chose stillness instead of spectacle, showing that His love doesn't need to shout—it is steady, gentle, and strong.

He came in simplicity. No palace or bed of gold—just rough straw and the tender care of His parents. Mary cradled Him gently, wrapping Him in soft cloths, her tired eyes glowing with joy. Joseph stayed close, making sure the manger was safe, his hands steady even as his heart trembled with wonder. God's glory doesn't need riches; it shines brightest in the ordinary places where we live and play.

And He came in smallness. Not as a warrior or a king with armies, but as a baby wrapped tightly in His mother's arms. God's strength is found in humility, not power.

So when you are quiet, when you do something simple, or when you feel small—remember that Jesus chose the same. Even your smallest acts of kindness or love can carry His light into the world.

Pause now. Breathe deeply. Let awe fill your chest.

Yesterday, you felt creation grow quiet, hushed in wonder as the Word who is light, life, and love drew near. Today, you find yourself at the edge of Bethlehem, the streets hushed beneath silver light. On the wind drifts the faintest sound—so small you wonder if you imagined it.

Something holy has begun, though hidden still from the world's eyes.

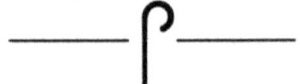

Father, thank You for sending Jesus so gently, so humbly, and so near. Thank You that He chose silence instead of noise, simplicity instead of splendor, and smallness instead of power—just so He could be with us. Fill my heart with wonder tonight, and help me see that even in quiet, ordinary, little moments, You are close through Him. I praise You for the gift of His birth. In Jesus' name. Amen.

Jesus, You came in silence, simplicity, and smallness. Your quiet arrival changed the world forever.

Day 23: Wrapped in Swaddling Clothes

"She wrapped him in cloths and placed him in a manger." — Luke 2:7b

*F*eel the gentle whisper of a warm breeze wrapping around you, like a soft blanket woven from the sky itself. Close your eyes slowly and take a deep breath, as if you're breathing in the clean scent of cotton drying in the sun, mixed with wildflowers in a summer meadow. Let your body rest in stillness, like a tiny seed safe beneath the soil, hidden but cared for.

Now imagine Mary's hands—gentle, tired, but steady—as she carefully lifts her newborn Son. Slowly, lovingly, she takes strips of cloth and wraps them around Him, snug and safe. The swaddling cloths are soft, but plain. Not robes of a king, not garments of gold or silk—just simple fabric, wrapping heaven's treasure in earthly humility. Feel how snug, how safe, how tender it is—like the gentlest hug you've ever known.You wrapped Yourself in love to hold my heart.

Look again at those tiny hands tucked inside the folds. Hands that one day will touch the sick and heal them. Hands that will lift the broken, feed the hungry, and finally carry the weight of a wooden cross. But tonight, they curl small and fragile, letting themselves be held. The One who created the heavens allowed Himself to be wrapped. The King of kings made Himself small enough to need care. That is the mystery of the swaddling cloths—not just fabric around a child, but God's love choosing to come close, bound to us in weakness so He could carry us forever in strength.

Now imagine yourself wrapped in a blanket like that—soft, warm, and steady. Not just any blanket, but the love of Jesus, wrapping around you like arms that never let go. When you feel scared at night, lying in the dark and wishing someone was close—imagine those swaddling cloths around you. Jesus is there, whispering, "You are not alone. I am with you." When you feel left out or pushed aside—remember the gentle wrapping of His love. He holds you steady, reminding you, "You are mine. I love you." When worries crowd your mind, making you feel small or unseen, picture yourself tucked into those folds, snug and safe. His love covers you—stronger than every fear, kinder than every hurt. Jesus' wrapping isn't just cloth—it's His very presence around you. Always holding. Always protecting. Always reminding you: "I am here. I will never leave you."

Yesterday, the night grew holy and still—the moment drew near. Today, you move closer through quiet streets and shadowed doorways. Every step feels wrapped in wonder as love waits for you.

Father, thank You for sending Jesus to be wrapped in such humility and love. Through Him, cover me with Your peace when I feel anxious or forgotten. Remind me that even when I feel small, Your strength surrounds me and holds me safe. I praise You for love that never loosens its grip. In Jesus' name. Amen.

Jesus was wrapped in swaddling cloths; His love now wraps around me forever. Today I will "wrap" others in kindness, comfort, and care.

(For parents — tomorrow's celebration prep)
Parents, please print the **Journey to the Manger Certificate** today (one per child). Slip it into an envelope, roll it like a scroll, or tie with a ribbon—and keep it hidden until Day 25.

Day 24: No Room at the Inn

"There was no guest room available for them." —Luke 2:6

T ake a deep, gentle breath in... feel the cool night air swirl inside you, like starlight slipping into your lungs. Hold it softly for a moment... now exhale, releasing every tight knot and worry.

Imagine yourself walking beside Mary and Joseph through the crowded streets of Bethlehem. The night sky above is glittering with stars, each one like a candle hung in heaven's window. But down here on earth, the streets are noisy and cramped. Donkeys bray, merchants call, children dart between legs, and doors swing open and shut. The smell of bread drifts from ovens, but the smell of dust and sweat clings too.

You watch as Joseph knocks on a door. A lantern flickers, a face peers out, and the words fall like stones: "No room." Another door—"No room." Another—"No room."

Can you feel the sting of those words? It's not just that the houses are full. It's that the doors close right in front of them. Have you ever felt that sting? Maybe you wanted to play a game, but the kids said, "You can't." Maybe you wanted to sit with a group, but they said, "Not here." Maybe even a brother, sister, or close friend turned away. Rejection feels sharp, like a splinter in your chest. It feels heavy, like carrying a bag of rocks no one else can see.

Take a slow breath in... and as you breathe out, imagine placing that ache into God's hands.

When the world says no to you, Jesus still says yes. Even when people close their doors, Jesus never will. He knows what rejection feels like, because He was rejected too—on this very night, when there was no guest room for Him. But unlike Bethlehem, His heart is always open for you. He will never drive you away. He will never pack up and leave. He will stay, right here, no matter what.

So if friends leave you out, or classmates ignore you, or even family hurts your heart—Jesus stays. Whisper it softly: *"Jesus, thank You for never rejecting me. Thank You for staying."*

When people say no to Jesus, you can still help Him find a yes. That night in Bethlehem, door after door shut in Mary and Joseph's face. *"No room,"* they were told, again and again. And even now, the same thing happens to Jesus. Every time someone hears the good news and says, *"Not for me,"* it's like another door in Bethlehem closing. Every time a heart is too crowded with pride, fear, or distractions, it's just like the streets of Bethlehem saying, *"No room."*

Can you imagine the ache He feels each time? The same ache you've felt when someone turned you away, He feels too.

But here's the miracle: because Jesus has made His home in you, you can help Him. You can be His open door in the world. Every kind word, every act of love, every moment you share Him—it's like swinging a door wide for someone else to welcome Jesus in.

It must have been hard for Mary and Joseph—door after door shutting in their faces. But they didn't give up. They didn't throw their hands in the air or stop in the street. Step by step, they kept moving, trusting God to provide. And He did. It wasn't the place they dreamed of. It wasn't grand or comfortable. But it was enough—and because Jesus was there, it became holy.

Sometimes you may feel the same. A door shuts in your face, or something doesn't go the way you hoped. You can feel like giving up, or blaming, or doing something wrong out of frustration. But remember Mary and Joseph. There is always another way. God always makes room, even if it's smaller or different than what you wanted. And wherever Jesus is, even the humblest place becomes full of glory.

Yesterday, you saw Jesus wrapped in swaddling cloths—heaven's love made small, humble, and near.

Today, you've seen closed doors and heavy hearts, but also the courage to keep going. The path is turning now, leading toward a hidden place where God's promise will be cradled. The night grows quieter. Something holy is just ahead... but still unseen.

Father, thank You for never rejecting me. Thank You that even when others shut me out, You open wide Your arms. When my heart feels heavy, remind me of the welcome You give through Jesus. Give me courage, like Mary and Joseph, to keep walking forward and trusting Your plan. And let my life be an open door where others can meet Jesus too. I praise You for Your love that never leaves. In Jesus' name. A men.

Jesus has made His home in me. With His love, I will keep moving, keep trusting, and keep opening doors for Him.

(*For parents — tomorrow's celebration prep*)Parents, please print the **Journey to the Manger Certificate** today (one per child). Slip it into an envelope, roll it like a scroll, or tie with a ribbon—and keep it hidden until Day 25.

Day 25 — Christ the Lord Is Born: The Moment Everything Changed

"And they came with haste, and found Mary, and Joseph, and the babe lying in a manger." — Luke 2:16

T ake a slow, deep breath in...Feel the crisp night air fill your lungs. Hold it... now breathe out softly, like letting a hush settle over a holy place.You've walked so far—through gardens and promises, under starry skies and quiet fields—and now you are here. Lantern light warms the wooden beams. Straw rustles under your feet. The air smells of hay and night. Something inside you whispers: **This is the place.**

There in the manger lies a baby, wrapped and resting. At first it looks simple—just a child on an ordinary night. But then your heart begins to pound.*The One in the manger is the Gift—God with us—for me.*This is not a small moment. This is the page where history turns.Before this night, the world was groaning. Sin had wrapped its chains around every heart. Darkness ruled like a shadow that would not lift. People tried to be good, but they could not break free. Promises were made, sacrifices offered, but the world still waited—longed—for Someone who could save.And then—on this night—it happened. The cry of a newborn cut through the silence of centuries. God stepped down into the danger, into the brokenness, into the darkness itself. The Savior had come. What no one could fix, He came to make whole. What no one could carry, He came to bear. From this moment on, nothing would ever be the same.

Come closer to the wood. Smell the sweet hay. **This is a feeding place**—a table for hungry ones. Animals do not argue here about who is worthy; they simply come and are fed. And here, in the very spot where food belongs, lies Jesus. It is as if God set His own table and placed His Gift upon it and whispered to the whole world, *Come and eat.*

Later, Jesus will say, "I am the bread of life," and that His flesh is true food, given "for the life of the world." He gave His body on the cross so our hearts could have real life with God. We don't bite Him with our teeth; we **receive** Him with trust. We take in His words. We remember Him at the Lord's Table with bread and cup. We let His life become our life. When we say *yes* to Him, it's like taking living bread into the empty places of our souls. *The manger is God's table, and Jesus is the Bread given for me.*

See how low the manger is—right at the ground where knees bend. Not a throne you must admire from far away. Not a high place that shuts small people out. It is low so the lowly can come. It is ordinary so ordinary hearts won't be afraid. The Highest One chose the lowest place so

anyone can draw near—children and kings, shepherds and travelers, the known and the unnoticed.

And look—the manger is open. No lid. No lock. **Love made room.** This open trough is like God's open door. "Him that cometh to Me I will in no wise cast out." No one who comes thirsty is turned away. Not for being too new or too late; not for being too poor or too rich; not for having questions or tears. The welcome stands: *Come and eat.*

What happens when you eat this Bread? Life happens. Forgiveness settles you. Peace rests on you. Strength grows inside you where fear used to live. Eternal life begins now—life with Jesus that never ends. And there is always enough. You cannot empty this table. You can share and share and share, and the Bread of Life is still more.

How do we come to the manger-table today? We **believe** His words and **receive** His love. We **listen** to Scripture and let it feed us. We **pray** and open the empty places to Him. We **remember** Him with the bread and the cup when we gather with God's people. Every little *yes* is a bite of living bread for your heart.

Close your eyes softly, **like drawing soft curtains**. In your imagination, kneel by the manger and hold out your hands as if receiving a small piece of bread. Whisper, "Jesus, You are my Bread of Life." Place your hand over your heart and breathe in slow, letting His nearness fill every empty place.

The angels cannot hold their song: "Glory to God in the highest! Peace on earth!" Stars seem to tremble with joy. And you are standing inside the story, eyes wide, realizing you have stepped into the very moment the whole world changed—and it happened **at a** manger. Let this sink deep: Jesus did not only come for the world—He came for **you**. Unto **you** a Savior is born. Unto **you** peace has come. Unto **you** love has arrived and will not leave. Close your eyes softly, **like drawing soft curtains**. Picture Him not only in Bethlehem's manger but right here with you. Hear His whisper in your heart: "I am here. I came for you. I am walking with you." Take one more gentle breath... and let His peace wrap you like the warmest blanket. Let that peace move your hands and words toward kindness today.

Yesterday, you saw doors closing and hearts turning away, but still Mary and Joseph kept going—trusting God to make room.**Today,** you kneel at the manger-table—Jesus, the Bread of Life, welcomes you to come and eat.

Father, thank You for setting a table for hungry hearts and giving us Jesus, the Bread of Life. Let His life feed my soul, steady my steps, and make me generous so I share Him with others. Keep my heart low and open, like the manger, so anyone near me can find room to come close to You. I praise You for such a Gift. In Jesus' name. Amen.

Jesus, the Bread of Life, came low to feed my heart and never turn me away. Today I will come and eat—and make room so others can come close too.

(For parents — awarding moment)

1. Dim the lights; light a candle or lantern if you have

one.

2. Read Luke 2:16 aloud together.

3. Hand your child the **Journey to the Manger Certificate** and say: "You completed the Journey to the Manger. Jesus came near—for you."

4. Child writes name and today's date.

5. Speak a short blessing over your child: "May the Lord keep your heart close to Jesus, the Bread of Life."

6. Child reads the declaration out loud; family echoes: "Christ the Lord is born. He is here."

7. Display the certificate for Christmas week (optional: snap a photo for loved ones).

Day 26 — His Light in Our Lives

"Ye are the light of the world. A city that is set on an hill cannot be hid." — Matthew 5:14

Take a long, slow breath with me now... Breathe in deeply, the night air cool and still, settling into your chest like peace finding its place. Hold it softly, as if cupping a fragile flame in your hands. Now release it, and as you exhale, let the rush and weight of the day fall away.

Now picture your heart as a home. Strong walls, steady roof, windows open and waiting. This is not an empty house, not a place hoping for someone to visit. No—Jesus already dwells here. The Prince of Peace rests by the fire. The Wonderful Counselor sets His lamp upon the table. The Everlasting Father guards the doorway. The Mighty God holds the frame steady with His strength. Every room carries the presence of the King of Glory.

But look closer. Without even noticing, the rooms begin to crowd. Worries stack in corners like boxes piled too high. Fears press close like heavy furniture blocking the windows. Doubts pull curtains tight, dimming the glow that longs to spill out. The air grows heavy. The space feels smaller. Yet He does not leave. His presence does not shift with the shadows.

Breathe again. Slowly in. Slowly out.

As you breathe, picture yourself clearing the space. One box lifted. One curtain pulled back. One chair gently moved aside. With each motion, the light grows stronger. Warmth spreads further. Shadows retreat. And His voice, quiet but steady, whispers: "*I am here. Let Me shine in every corner.*"

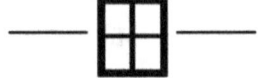

Suddenly this is not just a home. It is a beacon. Like a city set high on a hill, glowing in the night. His light within you cannot be hidden. Through the windows of your words, through the doors of your kindness, through the paths of your everyday steps—His light flows outward.

Others see it. They may not always have the words for it, but they recognize hope burning steady in you.

Stay here a moment in this vision. Feel His light filling every room, driving out the heaviness. Smell the fragrance of joy rising in the air. Hear the hum of peace like a gentle song moving through the walls. This is Christmas—not only the Light born in Bethlehem long ago, but the Light shining in you today.

The night of His birth has passed, but His light has not faded.

Today, that same light lives in you—a light the world cannot put out.

Father, thank You that Jesus, the Light of the world, has chosen to dwell in me. Thank You that no shadow can drive Him away, no clutter can push Him out, no darkness can overcome His glow. Teach me to make room for Him each day—to draw back the curtains, to lift away the weights, to welcome His presence into every corner of my life. Shine through me, Lord, so that others may see Your peace, Your joy, and Your love reflected in all I do. I give You thanks and praise, in Jesus' name. Amen.

I am a city on a hill, filled with His light. His peace, His joy, His love shine through me into the world.

Day 27 — Living Like Jesus Came to Stay

"Christ in you, the hope of glory." —
Colossians 1:27

T ake a long, slow breath with me now... Breathe in deeply, letting the cool, quiet air fill your lungs completely. Hold it softly, as if cradling a fragile flame... then breathe out slowly, releasing every trace of tension, every worry, every noise from your day. Let your body grow still, your mind settle like calm water, your heart open wide.

Imagine a warm, cozy home built just for you—a place where light spills through every window, where the walls echo with peace, and every corner holds quiet joy. This is your heart. And God has chosen to make it His home. He does this through the Holy Spirit, who lives in you.

Christmas is not just about Jesus being born in Bethlehem long ago. It is about His Spirit being born in you now. Jesus came into the world, but He didn't stop there—He sent the Holy Spirit so He could stay with you, forever.

The Bible says: "Christ in you, the hope of glory." We experience that truth through the Spirit who lives inside us. Not just beside you. Not just near you. But within you—your constant Friend, your quiet Teacher, your closest Companion.

Do you remember back on Day 3, when you opened your heart and welcomed the Holy Spirit to come in? That wasn't pretend. That was real. From that moment on, He has lived inside you. And now you can be sure: His home is your heart, and He will never leave.

Think about it: when loneliness tries to settle in your chest like a heavy shadow, you are not alone. You can whisper, "*Holy Spirit, I feel lonely. Thank You that You are here with me.*" And as you remember His presence, He fills that silence with comfort.

When someone hurts your feelings at school, or says something unkind, you can talk to Him: "*Holy Spirit, look at what they said to me. What should I do?*" And if you listen quietly, He will nudge your heart toward peace, kindness, and courage.

When you're unsure what step to take, even in little things, you can pause and ask: "*Holy Spirit, guide me. What would please You?*" And He will help you see what is good and true.

This is not imagination only—it is real. He hears. He answers. He stays. He speaks.

Take another slow breath... breathe in His nearness. Breathe out the thought that you are ever truly alone. The Spirit of God lives inside you—like a steady flame glowing in the center of your heart.

This flame is not small. It fills you with peace that anchors your soul, joy that bubbles up even on hard days, and love that reaches beyond yourself to others. If you stop and listen, you will hear His whisper guiding you, comforting you, reminding you: "I *am here. You belong to God.*"

Yesterday, you carried His light as a city on a hill. Today, you know the Holy Spirit lives within you—helping you, teaching you, guiding you every step.

This is Christmas—not only Jesus born into the world long ago, but His Spirit alive in you now.

My Father in heaven, thank You for sending the Holy Spirit to live in me. Thank You that I am never alone, because You are always with me. Teach me to talk with You about my fears, my joys, and even the little things in my day. Help me to listen when You whisper back, so I can walk in Your wisdom, peace, and love. I give You all my praise and thanks. In Jesus' name. Amen.

The Holy Spirit lives in me, guiding my thoughts, words, and steps. I will talk with Him, listen for His voice, and live knowing He has come to stay.

Day 28 — Giving More Than Gifts

"It is more blessed to give than to receive."
— Acts 20:35

*T*ake a long, slow breath with me now... Breathe in deeply, letting the cool, quiet air fill your lungs completely. Hold it gently, as if cradling a fragile flame... then breathe out slowly, releasing every trace of tension, every worry, every noise from your busy day. Let your body grow still, your mind settle like calm water, your heart open wide.

Imagine the soft crackle of a fire on a chilly winter evening. The flames dance warmly, sending golden light flickering across the walls of a cozy room. Outside, the world is hushed, blanketed in snow and silence. Inside, there is warmth—not just from the fire, but from hearts alive with love, ready to give.

Think about Christmas morning—the joy of unwrapping presents. The crinkle of shiny paper, the rustle of ribbon, the surprise sparkling in your eyes. Gifts come in all shapes and sizes—some loud and colorful, others quiet and small.

But listen closely—Jesus whispers a secret: "It is more blessed to give than to receive." The deepest joy isn't in how many presents you open, but in the love you release from your heart.

Picture your heart as a gift box, glowing with light. Inside is a treasure that never fades, never breaks, never wears out. You give this gift when you sit with someone who feels lonely, when you speak a kind word to a friend, when you help without being asked, when you smile at a stranger who needs hope. Even saying "thank you" or cheering someone on is a gift.

Not every time you feel like giving is the Spirit's whisper, but sometimes He does nudge you—quietly saying, *"Go share that,"* or *"Offer a kind word now."* And whether it's His prompting or your own choice to give in love, the Holy Spirit is always glad. Every time you share kindness, encouragement, or generosity, His heart is proud, because He sees Jesus shining through you.

Imagine this: you share your toy with your little brother, even though you wanted to keep it to yourself. The Holy Spirit smiles. Or you notice a classmate sitting alone and you walk over to say, *"Want to play with me?"* The Spirit is glad. Or someone offends you and instead of snapping back, you whisper in your heart, *"Holy Spirit, help me."* Then you choose kind words. In moments like these, He rejoices, because you are living like Jesus.

Giving like Jesus is not keeping score. It isn't about what you get back. It is the joy of pouring out kindness, patience, and care simply because love overflows in you.

Imagine that love like a river—clear, strong, unstoppable. Every time you give, you don't lose from the river. It grows deeper, wider, stronger.

For this is the way of Jesus. He gave the greatest gift—His very life—wrapped in sacrifice, tied with joy, given not for a moment but forever. His giving was full, free, and unstoppable.

Take a deep breath... breathe in the joy of giving. Breathe out the fear that whispers, "*I don't have enough.*"

Feel that river of love flowing through your heart, filling you with courage and peace. Imagine the ripples your giving creates—gentle waves spreading outward, touching lives farther than you can see.

What would it feel like to live each day with a heart ready to give? What light would shine through you if giving became your way of life?

Yesterday, you learned that the Spirit dwells within you. Today, you see His joy whenever you live with a giving heart.

This is Christmas—not only the gift God gave in His Son, but His Spirit rejoicing as His love flows through you.

My Father and my Lord, thank You for giving the greatest gift of all—Your Son, Your love, Yourself. Thank You that Your Spirit lives in me, guiding me and delighting when I give in love. Teach me to live with a heart that overflows in kindness, generosity, and joy. Let my words bring hope, my hands bring help, and my life shine with the Spirit's gladness. I give You all praise and thanks. In Jesus' name. Am en.

I am blessed to give, for Christ's love flows through me. I will live with a generous heart, making the Holy Spirit glad as His love shines through me.

Day 29 — Peace That Stays

"The peace of God, which passeth all understanding, shall keep your hearts and minds through Christ Jesus." — Philippians 4:7

T ake a slow, deep breath with me now... Breathe in deeply, as if drawing cool, steady air straight into your heart. Hold it gently... then breathe out slowly, letting your shoulders drop and your mind grow quiet. Feel the calm begin to settle, like snowflakes drifting down on a silent night.

Picture yourself standing in a quiet field under a blanket of stars. The world around you is hushed. No rushing, no noise, no stress—just stillness. This is the peace God promises. Not peace that comes and goes like a weather change, but peace that stays.

Sometimes life feels the opposite of peaceful. Your classroom gets noisy. Friends argue. A sibling snaps at you. Inside, your heart feels stirred up like a stormy sea, waves crashing, thoughts tumbling, nothing still. But God's Word says His peace can "guard" your heart and mind—like a strong wall that keeps the storm outside, unable to break through.

And this peace comes through the Holy Spirit, who lives inside you. When voices rise and everything feels loud, He whispers calm within you: "*I am here. Be still.*" When arguments pull at your heart like heavy waves, He steadies you so you don't get swept away. When frustration stirs like wind and thunder, He brings quiet to your thoughts, like a safe harbor in the storm.

Think about it: someone makes fun of you, and anger rises quickly. You pause and whisper, "*Holy Spirit, You are here. Give me calm.*" And peace fills the space where anger wanted to live.

Or you feel nervous before a test at school. Your stomach twists, your hands shake. You whisper, "*Holy Spirit, I feel afraid, but I know You are with me. Thank You for giving me courage.*" And suddenly you sense a calm strength that steadies you.

Or you lie in bed at night, shadows stretching across your room, and fear tries to knock at your door. You breathe deep and say, "*Holy Spirit, You are here. Your peace surrounds me.*" And you feel wrapped in His quiet presence, like a blanket no fear can tear away.

Take another breath in... and as you breathe out, imagine the Spirit's peace spreading through you, steady and strong, pushing back every storm inside. Hear His whisper: "*I am here. I am your peace. Let My calm guard your heart.*"

Yesterday, you learned the Spirit rejoices when you live with a giving heart. Today, you discover His peace is more than a feeling—it is His presence keeping you steady.

This is Christmas—not only peace announced by angels long ago, but peace alive in you through the Spirit today.

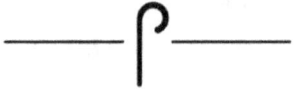

Father God, thank You for sending Your Spirit to live in me. Thank You that His peace is stronger than fear, louder than anger, and deeper than worry. Teach me to turn to Him when storms rise inside me. Help me to listen when He whispers calm, so I can walk steady and unafraid. I give You thanks for peace that never leaves. In Jesus' name. Amen.

The Holy Spirit fills me with peace that stays. I will listen to His whisper, walk in His calm, and let His peace shine through me.

Day 30 — What Will You Carry Forward?

"Forgetting those things which are behind, and reaching forth unto those things which are before, I press toward the mark for the prize of the high calling of God in Christ Jesus." —Philippians 3:13–14

T ake a long, slow breath with me now... Breathe in
deeply, feeling the crisp, gentle air fill your lungs
completely. Hold it softly, like cradling a tiny, flickering
flame... then breathe out slowly, releasing every worry, every
tightness, every heavy thought. Let your body grow quiet,
your mind settle like a still lake, your heart open wide like
a door waiting to welcome light.

Imagine you are preparing for a long journey. Before
you is a path stretching out beyond the horizon—new and
unknown. You reach for your pack for the road. It's meant
to carry what you need: your hopes, your dreams, your
faith.

But as you begin to pack, you notice some things are
too heavy for the road ahead. Worry sits like a stone at
the bottom, pressing down on your shoulders. Anger, like a
jagged rock, scratches and pokes at your heart. Fear tangles
itself like thick rope, wrapping tight and making every step
harder. And selfishness feels like stuffing your bag with
toys and treats you refuse to share—so full of "me, me, me"
that there's no room left for love.

Feel that weight for a moment. How does it press on
your shoulders? How does it slow your feet, cloud your
thoughts, or tighten your chest?

Now imagine standing at the edge of a new year, a fresh start stretching out before you. The old year is behind you like a sunset fading into night. The new day is dawning, full of promise and hope.

This is the perfect time to ask yourself: *What am I carrying that Jesus never asked me to carry?*

He doesn't want you to keep the stones of worry, the sharp edges of anger, the tangled ropes of fear, or the bag stuffed with selfishness. He asks you to set them down gently behind you, leaving them on the road that has passed.

What does He ask you to carry?

Faith—the bright lantern that lights the way through the darkest woods.

Hope—the steady staff that supports each step on uneven ground.

Love—the warm cloak that wraps you and others in kindness and peace.

And most of all, Jesus Himself—living in you by His Spirit—the sure Companion who walks with you through every twist and turn.

Take a slow, deep breath... breathe in faith, hope, and love. Breathe out fear, worry, anger, and selfishness.

Picture yourself opening your pack and taking out the heavy stones and tangled ropes. Feel the weight lift from your shoulders, your steps grow lighter, your spirit breathe easier.

You don't need to carry everything all at once. You don't need to know every turn ahead. You only need to keep pressing forward—one step at a time—trusting Jesus to lead the way.

Yesterday, you discovered the Spirit's peace guarding your heart. Today, you learn to leave behind what drags you down, and to carry only what Christ gives.

This is Christmas—not only the gift of Jesus born long ago, but the gift of freedom to walk forward with Him today.

My Father, thank You for walking with me on this journey. Thank You for lifting the weights I was never meant to carry and filling me instead with faith, hope, and love. I choose to release every burden into Your hands—fear, anger, worry, doubt, and selfishness that shouts *"me, me, me."* Fill me instead with kindness, generosity, and joy. Help me live each day with my eyes fixed on Jesus, my prize at the end and my Companion in every step. I give You thanks, I give You praise, and I give You my whole heart, now and always. In Jesus' name. Amen.

I leave behind fear, anger, worry, and selfishness, and I carry forward only what Christ gives. Jesus is my prize, my goal, and my guide, now and forever.

Day 31 — Jesus in Your New Year

"Behold, I make all things new." —
Revelation 21:5

Take a long, slow breath with me now... Breathe in deeply, feeling the cool, fresh air fill your lungs fully. Hold it softly, like cradling a small, glowing flame... then breathe out slowly, releasing every tension, every worry, every shadow from your heart. Let your body grow quiet, your mind settle like a still pond, your heart open wide like the first blossoms of spring.

Imagine holding a brand-new book—its cover bright and shiny, its pages crisp and clean. It smells of fresh paper and possibility. When something is new, it feels full of hope, like the first rays of morning light spilling gently over the hills, painting the world in gold and pink.

But as days pass, even the newest things begin to wear. Pages bend, colors fade, corners soften. And yet—there is one thing that never grows old, never fades, never wears out: Jesus' love for you.

His love is like a river flowing endlessly, carving paths of grace through the hardest places. His love is a fire burning steady, warm and bright through every season. His love is a song without end, carrying you even when the world grows silent.

The Bible says: "Behold, I make all things new." These words rise like a fresh sunrise breaking the horizon—promising renewal, hope, and fresh beginnings.

Imagine Jesus speaking these words straight to your heart: "*I can refresh your soul, reset your thoughts, renew your purpose—not just once a year, but every day.*"

Picture your heart as a garden—sometimes worn, sometimes weary. The soil may feel dry, the flowers wilted beneath worry. But Jesus, the gentle Gardener, kneels in your garden. Each day He waters with grace. New shoots press upward. New colors bloom. New fragrances fill the air with hope.

A new year with Jesus isn't about fixing everything at once. It isn't about perfection. It's about trust. Trust that He is already there—steady, patient, walking with you step by step, no matter what lies ahead.

Close your eyes for a moment. Feel the warmth of His hand resting on your shoulder—a quiet presence that says, "*You are not alone.*"

Breathe in His peace. Breathe out every fear.

Whisper softly: *Jesus, thank You for making all things new in me. Help me trust You more with each new day.*

Now picture the road before you—unfolding like a ribbon of light, steady beneath your feet. What will you carry into this year? What dreams will you hold close? What love will you choose to share?

Breathe in hope. Breathe out joy.

Yesterday, you learned to leave behind the weights that hold you down. Today, you step into the new year with Jesus making all things new.

This is Christmas—not only the celebration of His birth, but the joy of His love renewing you each day forward.

Father, thank You that every day with You begins new. Thank You that I don't have to cling to the past or fear the future, because You hold it all. As I step into the New Year, I place my hopes, my dreams, and my heart in Your hands. Renew me daily with Your love. Fill my days with Your peace. Let my life shine with Your grace so others may see Your goodness through me. I give You thanks, I give You praise, and I give You my whole heart—today and always. In Jesus' name. Amen.

With Jesus, my new year is filled with hope. He makes all things new—today, tomorrow, and forever.

31 Declarations of Christmas

1. *I am part of God's promise. Jesus is the light that shines forever. I walk toward the manger with hope, love, and peace in my heart.*

2. I have said yes to Jesus—He is my Savior and my Lord. Each day I will say yes to His Word and walk in His blessing. I am part of God's promise, moving forward with hope and joy. I am blessed to be a blessing. God's love in me reaches others with His light.

3. *God is not only with me — He lives in me by His Spirit. I will not be afraid.*

4. *I am a shining light. I carry Jesus' hope and love into the world.*

5. *God's Word is my safe place. His promises never fade, and His truth will guide me forever.*

6. *Jesus lives in my heart, and as I walk the garden path to the manger, God will use me to help others*

welcome Him too.

7. I carry the light of Jesus in my heart. My yes to Him makes me brave. Through my life, others will see His love and find the courage to say yes too.

8. I will trust God's plan, even when I don't understand it.

9. I will obey with a willing heart, and I will walk forward with courage, knowing God is with me every step.

10. Even when the road feels heavy, Jesus walks with me. I will keep moving forward, step by step, with Him.

11. God has not forgotten me. His timing is always perfect. I will trust Him while I wait.

12. I opened my heart wide to You, Lord, and Your Spirit lives in me. I carry Your light—gently, boldly, faithfully—through every ordinary step of my day.

13. Your glory fills my night, Lord. Your peace and joy guide every step I take.

14. Your promise stirs my wonder, Lord. Each step takes me nearer to the sign of Your love.

15. Your name is my shelter and my song, Jesus. I will whisper it, trust it, and carry it forever.

16. Jesus, You are the gift I could never earn. I will

treasure You always and let Your love shine through me.

17. Jesus, You are my peace. No storm, no noise, no fear can shake me when You are near.

18. Jesus, You are my joy and my song. Your joy shines in me, and I will share it wherever I go.

19. Jesus, You are my Savior forever— not just for a season, but for all my days.

20. Jesus, my Shepherd and my Lamb—You carried my sin and gave Yourself for me. I will follow Your voice and rest in Your love.

21. The Word became flesh and made His home among us. His presence changes everything—I am never alone.

22. Jesus, You came in silence, simplicity, and smallness. Your quiet arrival changed the world forever.

23. Jesus, You were wrapped in swaddling cloths of love— and now Your love wraps around me forever.

24. Jesus has made His home in me. With His love, I will keep moving, keep trusting, and keep opening doors for Him.

25. Jesus, the Bread of Life, came low to feed my heart and never turn me away. Today I will come and eat—and make room so others can come close too.

26. I am a city on a hill, filled with His light. His peace, His joy, His love shine through me into the world.

27. The Holy Spirit lives in me, guiding my thoughts, words, and steps. I will talk with Him, listen for His voice, and live knowing He has come to stay.

28. I am blessed to give, for Christ's love flows through me. I will live with a generous heart, making the Holy Spirit glad as His love shines through me.

29. The Holy Spirit fills me with peace that stays. I will listen to His whisper, walk in His calm, and let His peace shine through me.

30. I leave behind fear, anger, worry, and selfishness, and I carry forward only what Christ gives. Jesus is my prize, my goal, and my guide, now and forever.

31. With Jesus, my new year is filled with hope. He makes all things new—today, tomorrow, and forever.

Final Benediction — Jesus, Our Forever Gift

T ake one last deep breath with me now... Breathe in peace, breathe out praise.

We have journeyed together through these days of wonder, reflection, and light. We have stood at the manger, watched hope unfold, felt His presence draw near. We have breathed in His peace, His joy, His love—and we have carried Him into the rooms of our hearts, into the steps of our days.

And now, as this season closes and a new one begins, let your soul remember: Christmas is not only a day, not only a season, but a Person—Jesus, the One who came to stay.

He is the light that fills your home. He is the Shepherd who walks beside you. He is the Friend who never leaves you. He is the Hope who makes all things new.

So as you step forward into the days ahead, carry this truth like a flame that will not be extinguished: *Christ in you, the hope of glory.*

Rejoice always. Pray without ceasing. Give thanks in all things. Press forward to the prize. And walk in the love that never fails.

May your heart remain a manger where His presence rests. May your life shine like a lamp set on a hill. May your words be filled with kindness, your hands with giving, your days with gratitude, and your steps with courage.

And may you never forget that the same Jesus who was laid in a manger is the same Jesus who lives in you, walks with you, and makes all things new.

Breathe in His hope... Breathe out His love... And walk into this new year with your eyes lifted, your heart steady, and your soul at peace.

The Lord bless you and keep you. The Lord shine His face upon you and give you peace. The Lord go before you, behind you, and within you— Now and always, in Jesus' name. Amen.

Conclusion — Walking Forward with Jesus

We have traveled together through 31 days of wonder, reflection, and worship. From the angel's announcement to the light in the manger... From the whispers of shepherds in the night to the truth that *Christ lives in you, the hope of glory*... We have breathed in His peace, we have seen His love, we have heard His voice calling us nearer.

But the journey doesn't end here. Christmas is not the closing of a story—it is the beginning of a greater one. The same Jesus who came to Bethlehem is the Jesus who walks with you into every tomorrow.

What will you carry forward? Carry His light into your home. Carry His peace into your conversations. Carry His joy into your work and rest. Carry His love into every relationship. Carry His name upon your lips and His presence in your heart.

This is your call to action: **don't let Christmas fade when the decorations come down. Let Christ be the song you sing, the prayer you whisper, the hope you share.** Make space daily to breathe, to pause, to listen, to remember that He is with you.

The Scriptures you have read, the prayers you have whispered, the declarations you have spoken—keep them alive. Speak them over your life. Pray them in your home. Declare them over your year. Let these truths be planted like seeds, growing into a harvest of peace, joy, and love.

Above all, remember this: **Jesus is not a moment, He is forever. He is not a visitor, He is your dwelling. He is not only the Savior of the world, He is your Savior, your Shepherd, your Companion, your Friend.**

So as you step forward into the year ahead—whether the path is bright or dim, smooth or steep—you are not alone. Jesus, the Light of the world, walks with you. And with Him, every day is new.

Lift your eyes and whisper: *Jesus, You are my forever gift. You are my hope, my joy, my strength. I will walk with You always, shining Your light in all I do.*

May your days be filled with His peace. May your heart overflow with His joy. May your life reflect His love. And may you carry the miracle of Christmas into every day— Until the day you see Him face to face.

In Jesus' name, Amen.

Reader's Call to Action

As you step forward from these 31 days, don't leave the gift of Christmas behind. Carry Jesus with you into your every day by choosing these simple steps:

1. **Keep Meditating** – Take time each day to pause, breathe, and invite Jesus into your thoughts. Even a few quiet minutes can reset your heart in His presence.

2. **Speak Declarations of Truth** – Revisit the daily declarations in this book. Speak them out loud until they live in your spirit. Let your words shape your faith.

3. **Pray Without Ceasing** – Whisper short prayers throughout your day: "Jesus, be my peace. Jesus, guide my steps. Jesus, shine through me." Small prayers plant deep roots.

4. **Shine His Light** – Look for one way each day to give: a kind word, a smile, a helping hand, a listening ear. Every act of love is a reflection of Jesus in you.

5. **Carry the Christmas Spirit Forward** – Remember: Christmas is not a season you leave behind. It is a Person who lives in you. Walk each day with the truth that *Christ is your constant Companion.*

About the Author

"Only One Life" writes with a heart to help children know and love God from an early age. Through simple stories and biblical truths, their books give parents and teachers tools to guide children toward faith in Jesus and a strong foundation that will last a lifetime. Each story is written to spark imagination, open conversation, and lead young readers closer to the God who loves them.

www.ingramcontent.com/pod-product-compliance
Lightning Source LLC
Chambersburg PA
CBHW071748120626
46550CB00002B/704